KING LEAR

WILLIAM SHAKESPEARE

CONTENTS

DRAMATIS PERSONÆ

LEAR, king of Britain.
KING OF FRANCE.
DUKE OF BURGUNDY.
DUKE OF CORNWALL.
DUKE OF ALBANY.
EARL OF KENT.
EARL OF GLOUCESTER.
EDGAR, son to Gloucester.
EDMUND, bastard son to Gloucester.
CURAN, a courtier.
Old Man, tenant to Gloucester.
Doctor.
FOOL.
OSWALD, steward to Goneril.
A captain employed by Edmund.
Gentleman attendant on Cordelia.
Herald.
Servants to Cornwall.

GONERIL, daughter to Lear
REGAN, daughter to Lear
CORDELIA, daughter to Lear
Knights of Lear's train, Captains, Messengers,
    Soldiers, and Attendants.

SCENE: Britain.

ACT I.

SCENE I. KING LEAR'S PALACE.

(*ENTER* KENT, GLOUCESTER, *AND* EDMUND.)

KENT. I thought the king had more affected the Duke
of Albany than Cornwall.
GLOU. It did always seem so to us: but now, in the
division of the kingdom, it appears not which of the
dukes
he values most; for equalities are so weighed that
curiosity ₅
in neither can make choice of either's moiety.
KENT. Is not this your son, my lord?
GLOU. His breeding, sir, hath been at my charge: I
have so often blushed to acknowledge him that now
I am
brazed to it. ₁₀
KENT. I cannot conceive you.
GLOU. Sir, this young fellow's mother could:
whereupon
she grew round-wombed, and had indeed, sir, a son
for her
cradle ere she had a husband for her bed. Do you
smell a
fault? ₁₅
KENT. I cannot wish the fault undone, the issue of it
being so proper.

3

Glou. But I have, sir, a son by order of law,
  some year
elder than this, who yet is no dearer in my account:
  though
this knave came something saucily into the world
  before he $_{20}$
was sent for, yet was his mother fair; there was good
  sport
at his making, and the whoreson must be
  acknowledged.
Do you know this noble gentleman, Edmund?
Edm. No, my lord.
Glou. My lord of Kent: remember him hereafter as
  my $_{25}$
honourable friend.
Edm. My services to your lordship.
Kent. I must love you, and sue to know you better.
Edm. Sir, I shall study deserving.
Glou. He hath been out nine years, and away he
  shall $_{30}$
again. The king is coming.

(*Sennet. Enter one bearing a coronet,* King Lear,
Cornwall, Albany, Goneril, Regan, Cordelia, *and*
Attendants.)

Lear. Attend the lords of France and Burgundy,
  Gloucester.
Glou. I shall, my liege. Exeunt Gloucester and Edmund.)
Lear. Meantime we shall express our darker
  purpose.
Give me the map there. Know we have divided $_{35}$
In three our kingdom: and 'tis our fast intent
To shake all cares and business from our age,
Conferring them on younger strengths, while we
Unburthen'd crawl toward death. Our son of
  Cornwall,
And you, our no less loving son of Albany, $_{40}$
We have this hour a constant will to publish
Our daughters' several dowers, that future strife
May be prevented now. The princes, France and
  Burgundy,
Great rivals in our youngest daughter's love,

4

Long in our court have made their amorous
    sojourn, 45
And here are to be answer'd. Tell me, my daughters,
Since now we will divest us both of rule,
Interest of territory, cares of state,
Which of you shall we say doth love us most?
That we our largest bounty may extend 50
Where nature doth with merit challenge. Goneril,
Our eldest-born, speak first.

GON. Sir, I love you more than words can wield the
    matter,
Dearer than eye-sight, space and liberty,
Beyond what can be valued, rich or rare, 55
No less than life, with grace, health, beauty, honour,
As much as child e'er loved or father found;
A love that makes breath poor and speech unable;
Beyond all manner of so much I love you.

COR. Aside) What shall Cordelia do? Love, and be
    silent.60

LEAR. Of all these bounds, even from this line to this,
With shadowy forests and with champains rich'd,
With plenteous rivers and wide skirted meads,
We make thee lady. To thine and Albany's issue
Be this perpetual. What says our second daughter, 65
Our dearest Regan, wife to Cornwall? Speak.

REG. I am made of that self metal as my sister,
And prize me at her worth. In my true heart
I find she names my very deed of love;
Only she comes too short: that I profess 70
Myself an enemy to all other joys
Which the most precious square of sense possesses,
And find I am alone felicitate
In your dear highness' love.

COR. (Aside) Then poor Cordelia!
And yet not so, since I am sure my love's 75
More ponderous than my tongue.

LEAR. To thee and thine hereditary ever
Remain this ample third of our fair kingdom,
No less in space, validity and pleasure,
Than that conferr'd on Goneril. Now, our joy, 80
Although the last, not least, to whose young love
The vines of France and milk of Burgundy
Strive to be interess'd, what can you say to draw

A third more opulent than your sisters? Speak.
COR. Nothing, my lord. 85
LEAR. Nothing!
COR. Nothing.
LEAR. Nothing will come of nothing: speak again.
COR. Unhappy that I am, I cannot heave
My heart into my mouth: I love your majesty 90
According to my bond; nor more nor less.
LEAR. How, how, Cordelia! mend your speech a
  little,
Lest it may mar your fortunes.
COR. Good my lord,
You have begot me, bred me, loved me: I
Return those duties back as are right fit, 95
Obey you, love you, and most honour you.
Why have my sisters husbands, if they say
They love you all? Haply, when I shall wed,
That lord whose hand must take my plight shall
  carry
Half my love with him, half my care and duty: 100
Sure, I shall never marry like my sisters,
To love my father all.
LEAR. But goes thy heart with this?
COR. Ay, good my lord.
LEAR. So young, and so untender?
COR. So young, my lord, and true. 105
LEAR. Let it be so; thy truth then be thy dower:
For, by the sacred radiance of the sun,
The mysteries of Hecate, and the night;
By all the operation of the orbs
From whom we do exist and cease to be; 110
Here I disclaim all my paternal care,
Propinquity and property of blood,
And as a stranger to my heart and me
Hold thee from this for ever. The barbarous Scythian,
Or he that makes his generation messes 115
To gorge his appetite, shall to my bosom
Be as well neighbour'd, pitied and relieved,
As thou my sometime daughter.
KENT. Good my liege,—
LEAR. Peace, Kent!
Come not between the dragon and his wrath. 120
I loved her most, and thought to set my rest

On her kind nursery. Hence, and avoid my sight!
So be my grave my peace, as here I give
Her father's heart from her! Call *FRANCE*. Who stirs?
Call Burgundy. Cornwall and Albany, 125
With my two daughters' dowers digest this third:
Let pride, which she calls plainness, marry her.
I do invest you jointly with my power,
Pre-eminence and all the large effects
That troop with majesty. Ourself, by monthly
    course, 130
With reservation of an hundred knights
By you to be sustain'd, shall our abode
Make with you by due turns. Only we still retain
The name and all the additions to a king;
The sway, revenue, execution of the rest, 135
Beloved sons, be yours: which to confirm,
This coronet part betwixt you.
KENT. Royal Lear,
Whom I have ever honour'd as my king,
Loved as my father, as my master follow'd,
As my great patron thought on in my prayers,— 140
LEAR. The bow is bent and drawn; make from the
    shaft.
KENT. Let it fall rather, though the fork invade
The region of my heart: be Kent unmannerly,
When Lear is mad. What wouldst thou do, old man?
Think'st thou that duty shall have dread to speak, 145
When power to flattery bows? To plainness honour's
    bound,
When majesty stoops to folly. Reverse thy doom,
And in thy best consideration check
This hideous rashness: answer my life my
    judgement,
Thy youngest daughter does not love thee least; 150
Nor are those empty-hearted whose low sound
Reverbs no hollowness.
LEAR. Kent, on thy life, no more.
KENT. My life I never held but as a pawn
To wage against thy enemies, nor fear to lose it,
Thy safety being the motive.
LEAR. Out of my sight! 155
KENT. See better, Lear, and let me still remain
The true blank of thine eye.

Lear. Now, by Apollo,—
Kent. Now, by Apollo, king,
Thou swear'st thy gods in vain.
Lear. O, vassal! miscreant!

(Laying his hand on his sword.)

Alb. } Dear sir, forbear. 160
Corn.}
Kent. Do;
Kill thy physician, and the fee bestow
Upon the foul disease. Revoke thy doom;
Or, whilst I can vent clamour from my throat,
I'll tell thee them dost evil.
Lear. Hear me, recreant! 165
On thy allegiance, hear me!
Since thou hast sought to make us break our vow,
Which we durst never yet, and with strain'd pride
To come between our sentence and our power,
Which nor our nature nor our place can bear, 170
Our potency made good, take thy reward.
Five days we do allot thee, for provision
To shield thee from diseases of the world,
And on the sixth to turn thy hated back
Upon our kingdom: if on the tenth day following 175
Thy banish'd trunk be found in our dominions,
The moment is thy death. Away! By Jupiter,
This shall not be revoked.
Kent. Fare thee well, king: sith thus thou wilt
        appear,
Freedom lives hence, and banishment is here. 180
To *Cordelia*) The gods to their dear shelter take thee,
        maid,
That justly think'st and hast most rightly said!
To *Regan and Goneril*) And your large speeches may
        your deeds approve,
That good effects may spring from words of love.
Thus Kent, O princes, bids you all adieu; 185
He'll shape his old course in a country new. *(Exit.)*

(Flourish. Re-enter GLOUCESTER, *with* FRANCE, BURGUNDY, *and
Attendants.)*

8

Glou. Here's France and Burgundy, my noble lord.
Lear. My lord of Burgundy,
We first address towards you, who with this king
Hath rivall'd for our daughter: what, in the least, 190
Will you require in present dower with her,
Or cease your quest of love?
Bur. Most royal majesty,
I crave no more than what your highness offer'd,
Nor will you tender less.
Lear. Right noble Burgundy,
When she was dear to us, we did hold her so; 195
But now her price is fall'n. Sir, there she stands:
If aught within that little seeming substance,
Or all of it, with our displeasure pieced,
And nothing more, may fitly like your grace,
She's there, and she is yours.
Bur. I know no answer. 200
Lear. Will you, with those infirmities she owes,
Unfriended, new adopted to our hate,
Dower'd with our curse and stranger'd with our
    oath,
Take her, or leave her?
Bur. Pardon me, royal sir;
Election makes not up on such conditions. 205
Lear. Then leave her, sir; for, by the power that
    made me,
I tell you all her wealth. To *France*) For you, great
    king,
I would not from your love make such a stray,
To match you where I hate; therefore beseech you
To avert your liking a more worthier way 210
Than on a wretch whom nature is ashamed
Almost to acknowledge hers.
France. This is most strange,
That she, that even but now was your best object,
The argument of your praise, balm of your age,
Most best, most dearest, should in this trice of
    time 215
Commit a thing so monstrous, to dismantle
So many folds of favour. Sure, her offence
Must be of such unnatural degree
That monsters it, or your fore-vouch'd affection
Fall'n into taint: which to believe of her, 220

Must be a faith that reason without miracle
Could never plant in me.
COR. I yet beseech your majesty,—
If for I want that glib and oily art,
To speak and purpose not, since what I well intend,
I'll do't before I speak,—that you make known $_{225}$
It is no vicious blot, murder, or foulness,
No unchaste action, or dishonour'd step,
That hath deprived me of your grace and favour;
But even for want of that for which I am richer,
A still-soliciting eye, and such a tongue $_{230}$
As I am glad I have not, though not to have it
Hath lost me in your liking.
LEAR. Better thou
Hadst not been born than not to have pleased me
    better.
FRANCE. Is it but this, a tardiness in nature
Which often leaves the history unspoke $_{235}$
That it intends to do? My lord of Burgundy,
What say you to the lady? Love's not love
When it is mingled with regards that stand
Aloof from the entire point. Will you have her?
She is herself a dowry.
Bur. Royal Lear, $_{240}$
Give but that portion which yourself proposed,
And here I take Cordelia by the hand,
Duchess of Burgundy.
LEAR. Nothing: I have sworn; I am firm.
Bur. I am sorry then you have so lost a father $_{245}$
That you must lose a husband.
COR. Peace be with Burgundy!
Since that respects of fortune are his love,
I shall not be his wife.
FRANCE. Fairest Cordelia, that art most rich being
    poor,
Most choice forsaken, and most loved despised, $_{250}$
Thee and thy virtues here I seize upon:
Be it lawful I take up what's cast away.
Gods, gods! 'tis strange that from their cold'st
    neglect
My love should kindle to inflamed respect.
Thy dowerless daughter, king, thrown to my
    chance, $_{255}$

Is queen of us, of ours, and our fair France:
Not all the dukes of waterish Burgundy
Can buy this unprized precious maid of me.
Bid them farewell, Cordelia, though unkind:
Thou losest here, a better where to find. 260
LEAR. Thou hast her, France: let her be thine, for we
Have no such daughter, nor shall ever see
That face of hers again. Therefore be gone
Without our grace, our love, our benison.
Come, noble Burgundy. 265

(Flourish. Exeunt all but France, Goneril, Regan, and Cordelia.)

FRANCE. Bid farewell to your sisters.
COR. The jewels of our father, with wash'd eyes
Cordelia leaves you: I know you what you are;
And, like a sister, am most loath to call
Your faults as they are named. Use well our
      father: 270
To your professed bosoms I commit him:
But yet, alas, stood I within his grace,
I would prefer him to a better place.
So farewell to you both.
REG. Prescribe not us our duties.
GON. Let your study 275
Be to content your lord, who hath received you
At fortune's alms. You have obedience scanted,
And well are worth the want that you have wanted.
COR. Time shall unfold what plaited cunning hides:
Who cover faults, at last shame them derides. 280
Well may you prosper!
FRANCE. Come, my fair Cordelia.

(Exeunt France and Cordelia.)

GON. Sister, it is not a little I have to say of
      what most
nearly appertains to us both. I think our father will
      hence
to-night.
REG. That's most certain, and with you; next
      month 285
with us.

Gon. You see how full of changes his age is; the
    observation
we have made of it hath not been little: he always
loved our sister most; and with what poor
    judgement he hath
now cast her off appears too grossly. 290
Reg. 'Tis the infirmity of his age: yet he hath
    ever but
slenderly known himself.
Gon. The best and soundest of his time hath
    been but
rash; then must we look to receive from his age, not
    alone
the imperfections of long ingrafted condition, but
    therewithal 295
the unruly waywardness that infirm and choleric
years bring with them.
Reg. Such unconstant starts are we like to have from
him as this of Kent's banishment.
Gon. There is further compliment of leave-taking
    between 300
France and him. Pray you, let's hit together: if our
father carry authority with such dispositions as he
    bears,
this last surrender of his will but offend us.
Reg. We shall further think on 't.
Gon. We must do something, and i' the heat.
    (Exeunt.) 305

SCENE II. THE EARL OF GLOUCESTER'S CASTLE

(Enter Edmund, with a letter.)

Edm. Thou, nature, art my goddess; to thy law
My services are bound. Wherefore should I
Stand in the plague of custom, and permit
The curiosity of nations to deprive me,
For that I am some twelve or fourteen moonshines 5
Lag of a brother? Why bastard? wherefore base?
When my dimensions are as well compact,
My mind as generous and my shape as true,
As honest madam's issue? Why brand they us

With base? with baseness? bastardy? base, base? 10
Who in the lusty stealth of nature take
More composition and fierce quality
Than doth, within a dull, stale, tired bed,
Go to the creating a whole tribe of fops,
Got 'tween asleep and wake? Well then, 15
Legitimate Edgar, I must have your land:
Our father's love is to the bastard Edmund
As to the legitimate: fine word, 'legitimate!'
Well, my legitimate, if this letter speed
And my invention thrive, Edmund the base 20
Shall top the legitimate. I grow; I prosper:
Now, gods, stand up for bastards!

(ENTER GLOUCESTER.)

GLOU. Kent banish'd thus! and France in choler
    parted!
And the king gone to-night! subscribed his power!
Confined to exhibition! All this done 25
Upon the gad! Edmund, how now! what news?
EDM. So please your lordship, none.

(Putting up the letter.)

GLOU. Why so earnestly seek you to put up that
    letter?
EDM. I know no news, my lord.
GLOU. What paper were you reading? 30
EDM. Nothing, my lord.
GLOU. No? What needed then that terrible
    dispatch of
it into your pocket? the quality of nothing hath
    not such
need to hide itself. Let's see: come, if it be nothing, I
    shall
not need spectacles. 35
EDM. I beseech you, sir, pardon me: it is a letter from
my brother, that I have not all o'er-read; and for
    so much
as I have perused, I find it not fit for your o'er-
    looking.
GLOU. Give me the letter, sir.

EDM. I shall offend, either to detain or give it. The $_{40}$
contents, as in part I understand them, are to blame.
GLOU. Let's see, let's see.
EDM. I hope, for my brother's justification, he wrote
this but as an essay or taste of my virtue.
GLOU. (Reads) 'This policy and reverence of age
    makes $_{45}$
the world bitter to the best of our times; keeps our
    fortunes
from us till our oldness cannot relish them. I begin
    to find
an idle and fond bondage in the oppression of aged
    tyranny;
who sways, not as it hath power, but as it is suffered.
    Come
to me, that of this I may speak more. If our father
    would $_{50}$
sleep till I waked him, you should enjoy half his
    revenue for
ever, and live the beloved of your brother, EDGAR.'
Hum! Conspiracy!—'Sleep till I waked him, you
    should
enjoy half his revenue!'—My son Edgar! Had he
    a hand
to write this? a heart and brain to breed it in?
    When $_{55}$
came this to you? who brought it?
EDM. It was not brought me, my lord; there's the
    cunning
of it; I found it thrown in at the casement of my
    closet.
GLOU. You know the character to be your brother's?
EDM. If the matter were good, my lord, I durst
    swear $_{60}$
it were his; but, in respect of that, I would fain
    think it
were not.
GLOU. It is his.
EDM. It is his hand, my lord; but I hope his heart is
not in the contents. $_{65}$
GLOU. Hath he never heretofore sounded you in this
business?

EDM. Never, my lord: but I have heard him oft maintain

it to be fit, that, sons at perfect age, and fathers declining,

the father should be as ward to the son, and the [70] son manage his revenue.

GLOU. O villain, villain! His very opinion in the letter!

Abhorred villain! Unnatural, detested, brutish villain!

worse than brutish! Go, sirrah, seek him; ay, apprehend

him: abominable villain! Where is he? [75]

EDM. I do not well know, my lord. If it shall please

you to suspend your indignation against my brother till you

can derive from him better testimony of his intent, you

should run a certain course; where, if you violently proceed

against him, mistaking his purpose, it would make a great [80]

gap in your own honour and shake in pieces the heart of

his obedience. I dare pawn down my life for him that he

hath wrote this to feel my affection to your honour and to

no further pretence of danger.

GLOU. Think you so? [85]

EDM. If your honour judge it meet, I will place you

where you shall hear us confer of this and by an auricular

assurance have your satisfaction, and that without any further

delay than this very evening.

GLOU. He cannot be such a monster — [90]

EDM. Nor is not, sure.

GLOU. To his father, that so tenderly and entirely loves

him. Heaven and earth! Edmund, seek him out; wind me

into him, I pray you: frame the business after your own
wisdom. I would unstate myself, to be in a due resolution. 95

EDM. I will seek him, sir, presently, convey the business
as I shall find means, and acquaint you withal.

GLOU. These late eclipses in the sun and moon portend
no good to us: though the wisdom of nature can reason it
thus and thus, yet nature finds itself scourged by the sequent 100
effects: love cools, friendship falls off, brothers divide:
in cities, mutinies; in countries, discord; in palaces,
treason; and the bond cracked 'twixt son and father. This
villain of mine comes under the prediction; there's son
against father: the king falls from bias of nature; there's 105
father against child. We have seen the best of our time:
machinations, hollowness, treachery and all ruinous disorders
follow us disquietly to our graves. Find out this
villain, Edmund; it shall lose thee nothing; do it carefully.
And the noble and true-hearted Kent banished! his offence, 110
honesty! 'Tis strange. *(Exit.)*

EDM. This is the excellent foppery of the world, that
when we are sick in fortune—often the surfeit of our own
behaviour—we make guilty of our disasters the sun, the
moon and the stars: as if we were villains by necessity, 115
fools by heavenly compulsion, knaves, thieves and treachers,
by spherical predominance, drunkards, liars and adulterers,

by an enforced obedience of planetary influence;
and all that we are evil in, by a divine thrusting on:
     an admirable
evasion of whoremaster man, to lay his goatish $_{120}$
disposition to the charge of a star! My father
     compounded
with my mother under the dragon's tail, and my
     nativity
was under Ursa major; so that it follows I am
     rough and
lecherous. Tut, I should have been that I am, had the
maidenliest star in the firmament twinkled on my
     bastardizing. $_{125}$
Edgar—

(Enter EDGAR.)

And pat he comes like the catastrophe of the old
     comedy:
my cue is villanous melancholy, with a sigh like
     Tom o'
Bedlam. O, these eclipses do portend these divisions!
     fa,
sol, la, mi. $_{130}$
EDG. How now, brother Edmund! what serious
     contemplation
are you in?
EDM. I am thinking, brother, of a prediction I read
this other day, what should follow these eclipses.
EDG. Do you busy yourself about that? $_{135}$
EDM. I promise you, the effects he writ of succeed
unhappily; as of unnaturalness between the child
     and the
parent; death, dearth, dissolutions of ancient amities;
     divisions
in state, menaces and maledictions against king and
nobles; needless diffidences, banishment of friends,
     dissipation $_{140}$
of cohorts, nuptial breaches, and I know not what.
EDG. How long have you been a sectary
     astronomical?
EDM. Come, come; when saw you my father last?
EDG. Why, the night gone by.

EDM. Spake you with him? 145

EDG. Ay, two hours together.

EDM. Parted you in good terms? Found you no displeasure

in him by word or countenance?

EDG. None at all.

EDM. Bethink yourself wherein you may have offended 150

him: and at my entreaty forbear his presence till some

little time hath qualified the heat of his displeasure, which

at this instant so rageth in him that with the mischief of

your person it would scarcely allay.

EDG. Some villain hath done me wrong. 155

EDM. That's my fear. I pray you, have a continent

forbearance till the speed of his rage goes slower and, as I

say, retire with me to my lodging, from whence I will fitly

bring you to hear my lord speak: pray ye, go; there's my

key: if you do stir abroad, go armed. 160

EDG. Armed, brother!

EDM. Brother, I advise you to the best: go armed: I

am no honest man if there be any good meaning towards

you: I have told you what I have seen and heard; but

faintly, nothing like the image and horror of it: pray you, 165

away.

EDG. Shall I hear from you anon?

EDM. I do serve you in this business. *(Exit Edgar.)*

A credulous father, and a brother noble,

Whose nature is so far from doing harms 170

That he suspects none; on whose foolish honesty

My practices ride easy. I see the business.

Let me, if not by birth, have lands by wit:

All with me's meet that I can fashion fit. *(Exit.)*

SCENE III. THE DUKE OF ALBANY'S PALACE

(Enter Goneril and Oswald, her steward.)

GON. Did my father strike my gentleman for chiding
of his fool?
OSW. Yes, madam.
GON. By day and night he wrongs me; every hour
He flashes into one gross crime or other, 5
That sets us all at odds: I'll not endure it:
His knights grow riotous, and himself upbraids us
On every trifle. When he returns from hunting,
I will not speak with him; say I am sick:
If you come slack of former services, 10
You shall do well; the fault of it I'll answer.
OSW. He's coming, madam; I hear him. *(Horns
within.)*
GON. Put on what weary negligence you please,
You and your fellows; I'ld have it come to question:
If he distaste it, let him to our sister, 15
Whose mind and mine, I know, in that are one,
Not to be over-ruled. Idle old man,
That still would manage those authorities
That he hath given away! Now, by my life,
Old fools are babes again, and must be used 20
With checks as flatteries, when they are seen abused.
Remember what I tell you.
OSW. Very well, madam.
GON. And let his knights have colder looks
     among you;
What grows of it, no matter; advise your fellows so:
I would breed from hence occasions, and I shall, 25
That I may speak: I'll write straight to my sister,
To hold my very course. Prepare for dinner. *(Exeunt.)*

SCENE IV. A HALL IN THE SAME

(Enter Kent, disguised.)

KENT. If but as well I other accents borrow,
That can my speech defuse, my good intent
May carry through itself to that full issue

For which I razed my likeness. Now, banish'd Kent,
If thou canst serve where thou dost stand
    condemn'd, 5
So may it come, thy master whom thou lovest
Shall find thee full of labours.

(Horns within. Enter LEAR, Knights, and Attendants.)

LEAR. Let me not stay a jot for dinner; go get it ready.
(Exit an Attendant.) How now! what art thou?
KENT. A man, sir. 10
LEAR. What dost thou profess? What wouldst thou
with us?
KENT. I do profess to be no less than I seem; to serve
him truly that will put me in trust; to love him that is
    honest;
to converse with him that is wise and says little; to
    fear 15
judgement; to fight when I cannot choose, and to eat
    no fish.
LEAR. What art thou?
KENT. A very honest-hearted fellow, and as poor as
the king.
LEAR. If thou be as poor for a subject as he is for a 20
king, thou art poor enough. What wouldst thou?
KENT. Service.
LEAR. Who wouldst thou serve?
KENT. You.
LEAR. Dost thou know me, fellow? 25
KENT. No, sir; but you have that in your countenance
which I would fain call master.
LEAR. What's that?
KENT. Authority.
LEAR. What services canst thou do? 30
KENT. I can keep honest counsel, ride, run, mar a
curious tale in telling it, and deliver a plain message
bluntly: that which ordinary men are fit for, I am
    qualified
in, and the best of me is diligence.
LEAR. How old art thou? 35
KENT. Not so young, sir, to love a woman for
    singing,
nor so old to dote on her for any thing: I have years

on my

back forty eight.

LEAR. Follow me; thou shalt serve me: if I like thee no

worse after dinner, I will not part from thee yet. Dinner, 40

ho, dinner! Where's my knave? my fool? Go you, and

call my fool hither. *(Exit an Attendant.)*

(ENTER OSWALD.)

You, you, sirrah, where's my daughter?

Osw. So please you,— *(Exit.)*

LEAR. What says the fellow there? Call the clotpoll 45

back. *(Exit a Knight.)* Where's my fool, ho? I think the world's asleep.

(Re-enter Knight.)

How now! where's that mongrel?

KNIGHT. He says, my lord, your daughter is not well.

LEAR. Why came not the slave back to me when I 50 called him?

KNIGHT. Sir, he answered me in the roundest manner,

he would not.

LEAR. He would not!

KNIGHT. My lord, I know not what the matter is; but, 55

to my judgement, your highness is not entertained with that

ceremonious affection as you were wont; there's a great

abatement of kindness appears as well in the general dependants

as in the duke himself also and your daughter

LEAR. Ha! sayest thou so? 60

KNIGHT. I beseech you, pardon me, my lord, if I be mistaken; for my duty cannot be silent when I think

your highness wronged.

LEAR. Thou but rememberest me of mine own

conception:

I have perceived a most faint neglect of late; which I 65

have rather blamed as mine own jealous curiosity than as

a very pretence and purpose of unkindness: I will look

further into't. But where's my fool? I have not seen him

this two days.

Knight. Since my young lady's going into France, sir, 70

the fool hath much pined away.

Lear. No more of that; I have noted it well. Go you,

and tell my daughter I would speak with her. *(Exit an Attendant.)*

Go you, call hither my fool. *(Exit an Attendant.)*

(Re-enter Oswald.)

O, you sir, you, come you hither, sir: who am I, sir? 75

Osw. My lady's father.

Lear. My lady's father! my lord's knave: you whoreson

dog! you slave! you cur!

Osw. I am none of these, my lord; I beseech your pardon. 80

Lear. Do you bandy looks with me, you rascal?

(Striking him.)

Osw. I'll not be struck, my lord.

Kent. Nor tripped neither, you base foot-ball player.

(Tripping up his heels.)

Lear. I thank thee, fellow; thou servest me, and I'll love thee. 85

Kent. Come, sir, arise, away! I'll teach you differences:

away, away! If you will measure your lubber's length again,

tarry: but away! go to; have you wisdom? so.

(Pushes Oswald out.)

LEAR. Now, my friendly knave, I thank thee: there's
earnest of thy service. *(Giving Kent money.)* 90

(Enter Fool.)
FOOL. Let me hire him too: here's my coxcomb.

(Offering Kent his cap.)

LEAR. How now, my pretty knave! how dost thou?
FOOL. Sirrah, you were best take my coxcomb.
KENT. Why, fool?
FOOL. Why, for taking one's part that's out of
    favour: 95
nay, an thou canst not smile as the wind sits, thou'lt
    catch
cold shortly: there, take my coxcomb: why, this
    fellow hath
banished two on's daughters, and done the third a
    blessing
against his will; if thou follow him, thou must
    needs wear
my coxcomb. How now, nuncle! Would I had two
    coxcombs 100
and two daughters!
LEAR. Why, my boy?
FOOL. If I gave them all my living, I'ld keep my
    coxcombs
myself. There's mine; beg another of thy daughters.
LEAR. Take heed, sirrah; the whip. 105
FOOL. Truth's a dog must to kennel; he must be
    whipped
out, when Lady the brach may stand by the fire and
stink.
LEAR. A pestilent gall to me!
FOOL. Sirrah, I'll teach thee a speech. 110
LEAR. Do.
FOOL. Mark it, nuncle:
Have more than thou showest,
Speak less than thou knowest,
Lend less than thou owest, 115
Ride more than thou goest,

Learn more than thou trowest,
Set less than thou throwest;
Leave thy drink and thy whore,
And keep in-a-door, 120
And thou shalt have more
Than two tens to a score.

KENT. This is nothing, fool.

FOOL. Then 'tis like the breath of an unfee'd lawyer,
you gave me nothing for't. Can you make no use
of 125
nothing, nuncle?

LEAR. Why, no, boy; nothing can be made out of
nothing.

FOOL. *(To Kent)* Prithee, tell him, so much the rent of
his land comes to: he will not believe a fool. 130

LEAR. A bitter fool!

FOOL. Dost thou know the difference, my boy,
between
a bitter fool and a sweet fool?

LEAR. No, lad; teach me.

FOOL. That lord that counsell'd thee 135
To give away thy land,
Come place him here by me;
Do thou for him stand:
The sweet and bitter fool
Will presently appear;
The one in motley here, 140
The other found out there.

LEAR. Dost thou call me fool, boy?

FOOL. All thy other titles thou hast given away; that
thou wast born with. 145

KENT. This is not altogether fool, my lord.

FOOL. No, faith, lords and great men will not let
me; if
I had a monopoly out, they would have part
on't: and
ladies too, they will not let me have all the fool to
myself;
they'll be snatching. Give me an egg, nuncle, and I'll
give 150
thee two crowns.

LEAR. What two crowns shall they be?

FOOL. Why, after I have cut the egg in the middle and

eat up the meat, the two crowns of the egg. When thou

clovest thy crown i' the middle and gavest away both parts, 155

thou borest thine ass on thy back o'er the dirt: thou hadst

little wit in thy bald crown when thou gavest thy golden

one away. If I speak like myself in this, let him be whipped

that first finds it so.

(Singing) Fools had ne'er less wit in a year; 160
For wise men are grown foppish,
And know not how their wits to wear,
Their manners are so apish.

LEAR. When were you wont to be so full of songs, sirrah?

FOOL. I have used it, nuncle, ever since thou madest thy 165

daughters thy mother: for when thou gavest them the rod

and puttest down thine own breeches,

(Singing) Then they for sudden joy did weep,
And I for sorrow sung,
That such a king should play bo-peep, 170
And go the fools among.

Prithee, nuncle, keep a schoolmaster that can teach thy

fool to lie: I would fain learn to lie.

LEAR. An you lie, sirrah, we'll have you whipped.

FOOL. I marvel what kin thou and thy daughters are: 175

they'll have me whipped for speaking true, thou'lt have me

whipped for lying, and sometimes I am whipped for holding

my peace. I had rather be any kind o' thing than a fool:

and yet I would not be thee, nuncle; thou hast pared thy

wit o' both sides and left nothing i' the middle. Here
comes 180
one o' the parings.

(Enter Goneril.)

LEAR. How now, daughter! what makes that frontlet
on?
Methinks you are too much of late i' the frown.
FOOL. Thou wast a pretty fellow when thou hadst no
need to care for her frowning; now thou art an O
without 185
a figure: I am better than thou art now; I am a
fool, thou
art nothing. *(To Gon.)* Yes, forsooth, I will hold my
tongue; so your face bids me, though you say
nothing.
Mum, mum:
He that keeps nor crust nor crumb, 190
Weary of all, shall want some.
(Pointing to Lear) That's a shealed peascod.
GON. Not only, sir, this your all-licensed fool,
But other of your insolent retinue
Do hourly carp and quarrel, breaking forth 195
In rank and not to be endured riots. Sir,
I had thought, by making this well known unto you,
To have found a safe redress; but now grow fearful,
By what yourself too late have spoke and done,
That you protect this course and put it on 200
By your allowance; which if you should, the fault
Would not 'scape censure, nor the redresses sleep,
Which, in the tender of a wholesome weal,
Might in their working do you that offence
Which else were shame, that then necessity 205
Will call discreet proceeding.
FOOL. For, you know, nuncle,
The hedge-sparrow fed the cuckoo so long,
That it had it head bit off by it young.
So out went the candle, and we were left darkling.

210
LEAR. Are you our daughter?
GON. Come, sir,
I would you would make use of that good wisdom

Whereof I know you are fraught, and put away
These dispositions that of late transform you $_{215}$
From what you rightly are.
FOOL. May not an ass know when the cart draws the
horse? Whoop, Jug! I love thee.
LEAR. Doth any here know me? This is not Lear:
Doth Lear walk thus? speak thus? Where are his
    eyes? $_{220}$
Either his notion weakens, his discernings
Are lethargied—Ha! waking? 'tis not so.
Who is it that can tell me who I am?
FOOL. Lear's shadow.
LEAR. I would learn that; for, by the marks of
    sovereignty $_{225}$
knowledge and reason, I should be false persuaded
I had daughters.
FOOL. Which they will make an obedient father.
LEAR. Your name, fair gentlewoman?
GON. This admiration, sir, is much o' the savour $_{230}$
Of other your new pranks. I do beseech you
To understand my purposes aright:
As you are old and reverend, you should be wise.
Here do you keep a hundred knights and squires;
Men so disorder'd, so debosh'd and bold, $_{235}$
That this our court, infected with their manners,
Shows like a riotous inn: epicurism and lust
Make it more like a tavern or a brothel
Than a graced palace. The shame itself doth speak
For instant remedy: be then desired $_{240}$
By her that else will take the thing she begs
A little to disquantity your train,
And the remainder that shall still depend,
To be such men as may besort your age,
Which know themselves and you.
LEAR. Darkness and devils! $_{245}$
Saddle my horses; call my train together.
Degenerate bastard! I'll not trouble thee:
Yet have I left a daughter.
GON. You strike my people, and your disorder'd
    rabble
Make servants of their betters. $_{250}$

(ENTER ALBANY.)

27

LEAR. Woe, that too late repents,—*(To ALB.)* O, sir,
    are you come?
Is it your will? Speak, sir. Prepare my horses.
Ingratitude, thou marble-hearted fiend,
More hideous when thou show'st thee in a child
Than the sea-monster!
ALB. Pray, sir, be patient. ₂₅₅
LEAR. *(To Gon.)* Detested kite! thou liest.
My train are men of choice and rarest parts,
That all particulars of duty know,
And in the most exact regard support
The worships of their name. O most small fault, ₂₆₀
How ugly didst thou in Cordelia show!
That, like an engine, wrench'd my frame of nature
From the fix'd place, drew from my heart all love
And added to the gall. O Lear, Lear, Lear!
Beat at this gate, that let thy folly in *(Striking his
    head.)* ₂₆₅
And thy dear judgement out! Go, go, my people.
ALB. My lord, I am guiltless, as I am ignorant
Of what hath moved you.
LEAR. It may be so, my lord.
Hear, nature, hear; dear goddess, hear!
Suspend thy purpose, if thou didst intend ₂₇₀
To make this creature fruitful:
Into her womb convey sterility:
Dry up in her the organs of increase,
And from her derogate body never spring
A babe to honour her! If she must teem, ₂₇₅
Create her child of spleen, that it may live
And be a thwart disnatured torment to her.
Let it stamp wrinkles in her brow of youth;
With cadent tears fret channels in her cheeks;
Turn all her mother's pains and benefits ₂₈₀
To laughter and contempt; that she may feel
How sharper than a serpent's tooth it is
To have a thankless child! Away, away! *(Exit.)*
ALB. Now, gods that we adore, whereof comes this?
GON. Never afflict yourself to know the cause, ₂₈₅
But let his disposition have that scope
That dotage gives it.

(Re-enter LEAR.)

LEAR. What, fifty of my followers at a clap!
Within a fortnight!
ALB. What's the matter, sir?
LEAR. I'll tell thee. *(To Gon.)* Life and death! I am
   ashamed 290
That thou hast power to shake my manhood thus;
That these hot tears, which break from me perforce,
Should make thee worth them. Blasts and fogs upon
   thee!
The untented woundings of a father's curse
Pierce every sense about thee! Old fond eyes, 295
Beweep this cause again, I'll pluck ye out
And cast you with the waters that you lose,
To temper clay. Yea, is it come to this?
Let it be so: yet have I left a daughter,
Who, I am sure, is kind and comfortable: 300
When she shall hear this of thee, with her nails
She'll flay thy wolvish visage. Thou shalt find
That I'll resume the shape which thou dost think
I have cast off for ever: thou shalt, I warrant thee.

(Exeunt Lear, Kent, and Attendants.)

GON. Do you mark that, my lord? 305
ALB. I cannot be so partial, Goneril,
To the great love I bear you,—
GON. Pray you, content. What, Oswald, ho!
(To the Fool) You, sir, more knave than fool, after your
   master.
FOOL. Nuncle Lear, nuncle Lear, tarry; take the
   fool 310
with thee.
A fox, when one has caught her,
And such a daughter,
Should sure to the slaughter,
If my cap would buy a halter: 315
So the fool follows after, *(Exit.)*
GON. This man hath had good counsel: a hundred
   knights!
'Tis politic and safe to let him keep
At point a hundred knights: yes, that on every
   dream,
Each buzz, each fancy, each complaint, dislike, 320

He may enguard his dotage with their powers
And hold our lives in mercy. Oswald, I say!
ALB. Well, you may fear too far.
GON. Safer than trust too far:
Let me still take away the harms I fear,
Not fear still to be taken: I know his heart. 325
What he hath utter'd I have writ my sister:
If she sustain him and his hundred knights,
When I have show'd the unfitness,—

(Re-enter OSWALD.)

How now, Oswald!
What, have you writ that letter to my sister?
OSW. Yes, madam. 330
GON. Take you some company, and away to horse:
Inform her full of my particular fear,
And thereto add such reasons of your own
As may compact it more. Get you gone;
And hasten your return. *(Exit Oswald.)* No, no, my
    lord, 335
This milky gentleness and course of yours
Though I condemn not, yet, under pardon,
You are much more attask'd for want of wisdom
Than praised for harmful mildness.
ALB. How far your eyes may pierce I cannot tell: 340
Striving to better, oft we mar what's well.
GON. Nay, then—
ALB. Well, well; the event. *(Exeunt.)*

SCENE V. COURT BEFORE THE SAME

(Enter Lear, Kent, and Fool.)

LEAR. Go you before to Gloucester with these letters.
Acquaint my daughter no further with any thing
    you know
than comes from her demand out of the letter. If
    your diligence
be not speedy, I shall be there afore you.
KENT. I will not sleep, my lord, till I have delivered 5
your letter. *(Exit.)*
FOOL. If a man's brains were in's heels, were't not in

danger of kibes?

LEAR. Ay, boy.

FOOL. Then, I prithee, be merry; thy wit shall ne'er
go 10
slip-shod.

LEAR. Ha, ha, ha!

FOOL. Shalt see thy other daughter will use thee
kindly;

for though she's as like this as a crab's like an apple,
yet I

can tell what I can tell. 15

LEAR. Why, what canst thou tell, boy?

FOOL. She will taste as like this as a crab does to a

crab. Thou canst tell why one's nose stands i' the
middle

on's face?

LEAR. No. 20

FOOL. Why, to keep one's eyes of either side's nose,

that what a man cannot smell out he may spy into.

LEAR. I did her wrong—

FOOL. Canst tell how an oyster makes his shell?

LEAR. No. 25

FOOL. Nor I neither; but I can tell why a snail has a
house.

LEAR. Why?

FOOL. Why, to put's head in; not to give it away
to his

daughters, and leave his horns without a case. 30

LEAR. I will forget my nature.—So kind a father!—Be
my horses ready?

FOOL. Thy asses are gone about 'em. The reason why
the seven stars are no more than seven is a pretty
reason.

LEAR. Because they are not eight? 35

FOOL. Yes, indeed: thou wouldst make a good fool.

LEAR. To take 't again perforce! Monster ingratitude!

FOOL. If thou wert my fool, nuncle, I'ld have thee
beaten
for being old before thy time.

LEAR. How's that? 40

FOOL. Thou shouldst not have been old till thou
hadst
been wise.

LEAR. O, let me not be mad, not mad, sweet heaven!
Keep me in temper: I would not be mad!

(Enter Gentleman.)

How now! are the horses ready? 45
GENT. Ready, my lord.
LEAR. Come, boy.
FOOL. She that's a maid now and laughs at my
    departure
Shall not be a maid long, unless things be cut
    shorter.

(Exeunt.)

ACT II.

SCENE I. THE EARL OF GLOUCESTER'S CASTLE.

(Enter EDMUND and CURAN, meeting.)

EDM. Save thee, Curan.

CUR. And you, sir. I have been with your father, and
given him notice that the Duke of Cornwall and
    Regan his
duchess will be here with him this night.

EDM. How comes that? 5

CUR. Nay, I know not. You have heard of the news
abroad, I mean the whispered ones, for they are
    yet but
ear-kissing arguments?

EDM. Not I; pray you, what are they?

CUR. Have you heard of no likely wars toward,
    'twixt 10
the Dukes of Cornwall and Albany?

EDM. Not a word.

CUR. You may do then in time. Fare you well, sir.
    (Exit.)

EDM. The duke be here to-night? The better! best!
This weaves itself perforce into my business. 15
My father hath set guard to take my brother;
And I have one thing, of a queasy question,
Which I must act: briefness and fortune, work!
Brother, a word; descend: brother, I say!

(Enter EDGAR.)

My father watches: O sir, fly this place; ₂₀
Intelligence is given where you are hid;
You have now the good advantage of the night:
Have you not spoken 'gainst the Duke of Cornwall?
He's coming hither, now, i' the night, i' the haste,
And Regan with him: have you nothing said ₂₅
Upon his party 'gainst the Duke of Albany?
Advise yourself.
EDG. I am sure on't, not a word.
EDM. I hear my father coming: pardon me:
In cunning I must draw my sword upon you:
Draw: seem to defend yourself: now quit you well. ₃₀
Yield: come before my father. Light, ho, here!
Fly, brother. Torches, torches! So farewell.

(Exit Edgar.)

Some blood drawn on me would beget opinion

(Wounds his arm.)

Of my more fierce endeavour: I have seen drunkards
Do more than this in sport. Father, father! ₃₅
Stop, stop! No help?

(Enter GLOUCESTER, and Servants with torches.)

GLOU. Now, Edmund, where's the villain?
EDM. Here stood he in the dark, his sharp sword out,
Mumbling of wicked charms, conjuring the moon
To stand 's auspicious mistress.
GLOU. But where is he? ₄₀
EDM. Look, sir, I bleed.
GLOU. Where is the villain, Edmund?
EDM. Fled this way, sir. When by no means he
    could—
GLOU. Pursue him, ho!—Go after. *(Exeunt some
    Servants.)* 'By no means' what?
EDM. Persuade me to the murder of your lordship;
But that I told him the revenging gods ₄₅
'Gainst parricides did all their thunders bend,

Spoke with how manifold and strong a bond
The child was bound to the father; sir, in fine,
Seeing how loathly opposite I stood
To his unnatural purpose, in fell motion ₅₀
With his prepared sword he charges home
My unprovided body, lanced mine arm:
But when he saw my best alarum'd spirits
Bold in the quarrel's right, roused to the encounter,
Or whether gasted by the noise I made, ₅₅
Full suddenly he fled.
Glou. Let him fly far:
Not in this land shall he remain uncaught;
And found—dispatch. The noble duke my master,
My worthy arch and patron, comes to-night:
By his authority I will proclaim it, ₆₀
That he which finds him shall deserve our thanks,
Bringing the murderous caitiff to the stake;
He that conceals him, death.
Edm. When I dissuaded him from his intent
And found him pight to do it, with curst speech ₆₅
I threaten'd to discover him: he replied,
'Thou unpossessing bastard! dost thou think,
If I would stand against thee, could the reposure
Of any trust, virtue, or worth, in thee
Make thy words faith'd? No: what I should
        deny— ₇₀
As this I would; ay, though thou didst produce
My very character—I'ld turn it all
To thy suggestion, plot, and damned practice:
And thou must make a dullard of the world,
If they not thought the profits of my death ₇₅
Were very pregnant and potential spurs
To make thee seek it.'
Glou. Strong and fasten'd villain!
Would he deny his letter? I never got him.

                                        (Tucket within.)

Hark, the duke's trumpets! I know not why he
        comes.
All ports I'll bar; the villain shall not 'scape; ₈₀
The duke must grant me that: besides, his picture
I will send far and near, that all the kingdom

May have due note of him; and of my land,
Loyal and natural boy, I'll work the means
To make thee capable. 85

(Enter Cornwall, Regan, *and Attendants.)*

Corn. How now, my noble friend! since I came
   hither,
Which I can call but now, I have heard strange news.
Reg. If it be true, all vengeance comes too short
Which can pursue the offender. How dost, my lord?
Glou. O, madam, my old heart is crack'd, is
   crack'd! 90
Reg. What, did my father's godson seek your life?
He whom my father named? your Edgar?
Glou. O, lady, lady, shame would have it hid!
Reg. Was he not companion with the riotous knights
That tend upon my father? 95
Glou. I know not, madam: 'tis too bad, too bad.
Edm. Yes, madam, he was of that consort.
Reg. No marvel then, though he were ill affected:
'Tis they have put him on the old man's death,
To have the waste and spoil of his revenues. 100
I have this present evening from my sister
Been well inform'd of them, and with such cautions
That if they come to sojourn at my house,
I'll not be there.
Corn. Nor I, assure thee, Regan.
Edmund, I hear that you have shown your father 105
A child-like office.
Edm. 'Twas my duty, sir.
Glou. He did bewray his practice, and received
This hurt you see, striving to apprehend him.
Corn. Is he pursued?
Glou. Ay, my good lord.
Corn. If he be taken, he shall never more 110
Be fear'd of doing harm: make your own purpose,
How in my strength you please. For you, Edmund,
Whose virtue and obedience doth this instant
So much commend itself, you shall be ours:
Natures of such deep trust we shall much need: 115
You we first seize on.
Edm. I shall serve you, sir,

Truly, however else.
Glou. For him I thank your grace.
Corn. You know not why we came to visit you,—
Reg. Thus out of season, threading dark-eyed night:
Occasions, noble Gloucester, of some poise, 120
Wherein we must have use of your advice:
Our father he hath writ, so hath our sister,
Of differences, which I least thought it fit
To answer from our home; the several messengers
From hence attend dispatch. Our good old
    friend, 125
Lay comforts to your bosom and bestow
Your needful counsel to our business,
Which craves the instant use.
Glou. I serve you, madam:
Your graces are right welcome. *(Flourish. Exeunt.)*

SCENE II. BEFORE GLOUCESTER'S CASTLE

(Enter Kent and Oswald, severally.)

Osw. Good dawning to thee, friend: art of this
    house?
Kent. Ay.
Osw. Where may we set our horses?
Kent. I' the mire.
Osw. Prithee, if thou lovest me, tell me. 5
Kent. I love thee not.
Osw. Why then I care not for thee.
Kent. If I had thee in Lipsbury pinfold, I
    would make
thee care for me.
Osw. Why dost thou use me thus? I know thee
    not. 10
Kent. Fellow, I know thee.
Osw. What dost thou know me for?
Kent. A knave; a rascal, an eater of broken meats; a
base, proud, shallow, beggarly, three-suited,
    hundred-pound,
filthy, worsted-stocking knave; a lily-livered,
    action-taking 15
knave; a whoreson, glass-gazing, superserviceable,
    finical

rogue; one-trunk-inheriting slave; one that wouldst
be a
bawd in way of good service, and art nothing but
the composition
of a knave, beggar, coward, pandar, and the son
and heir of a mongrel bitch: one whom I will beat
into $_{20}$
clamorous whining, if thou deniest the least syllable
of thy
addition.

Osw. Why, what a monstrous fellow art thou, thus to
rail on one that is neither known of thee nor knows
thee!

Kent. What a brazen-faced varlet art thou, to deny $_{25}$
thou knowest me! Is it two days ago since I
tripped up
thy heels and beat thee before the king? Draw, you
rogue:
for, though it be night, yet the moon shines; I'll
make a
sop o' the moonshine of you: draw, you whoreson
cullionly
barber-monger, draw. *(Drawing his sword.)* $_{30}$

Osw. Away! I have nothing to do with thee.

Kent. Draw, you rascal: you come with letters
against
the king, and take vanity the puppet's part
against the
royalty of her father: draw, you rogue, or I'll so
carbonado
your shanks: draw, you rascal; come your ways. $_{35}$

Osw. Help, ho! murder! help!

Kent. Strike, you slave; stand, rogue; stand, you neat
slave, strike. *(Beating him.)*

Osw. Help, ho! murder! murder!

*(Enter EDMUND, with his rapier drawn, CORNWALL, REGAN,
GLOUCESTER, and Servants.)*

Edm. How now! What's the matter? *(Parting them.)* $_{40}$

Kent. With you, goodman boy, an you please: come,
I'll flesh you; come on, young master.

Glou. Weapons! arms! What's the matter here?

CORN. Keep peace, upon your lives;
He dies that strikes again. What is the matter? 45
REG. The messengers from our sister and the king.
CORN. What is your difference? speak.
OSW. I am scarce in breath, my lord.
KENT. No marvel, you have so bestirred your valour.
You cowardly rascal, nature disclaims in thee: a
    tailor made 50
thee.
CORN. Thou art a strange fellow: a tailor make
    a man?
KENT. Ay, a tailor, sir: a stone-cutter or a painter
could not have made him so ill, though he had
    been but
two hours at the trade. 55
CORN. Speak yet, how grew your quarrel?
OSW. This ancient ruffian, sir, whose life I have
    spared
at suit of his gray beard,—
KENT. Thou whoreson zed! thou unnecessary letter!
My lord, if you will give me leave, I will tread this
    unbolted 60
villain into mortar, and daub the walls of a jakes
with him. Spare my gray beard, you wagtail?
CORN. Peace, sirrah!
You beastly knave, know you no reverence?
KENT. Yes, sir; but anger hath a privilege. 65
CORN. Why art thou angry?
KENT. That such a slave as this should wear a sword,
Who wears no honesty. Such smiling rogues as these,
Like rats, oft bite the holy cords a-twain
Which are too intrinse to unloose; smooth every
    passion 70
That in the natures of their lords rebel;
Bring oil to fire, snow to their colder moods;
Renege, affirm, and turn their halcyon beaks
With every gale and vary of their masters,
Knowing nought, like dogs, but following. 75
A plague upon your epileptic visage!
Smile you my speeches, as I were a fool?
Goose, if I had you upon Sarum plain,
I'ld drive ye cackling home to Camelot.
CORN. What, art thou mad, old fellow? 80

Glou. How fell you out? say that.

Kent. No contraries hold more antipathy
Than I and such a knave.

Corn. Why dost thou call him knave? What is his fault?

Kent. His countenance likes me not. 85

Corn. No more perchance does mine, nor his, nor hers.

Kent. Sir, 'tis my occupation to be plain:
I have seen better faces in my time
Than stands on any shoulders that I see
Before me at this instant.

Corn. This is some fellow, 90
Who, having been praised for bluntness, doth affect
A saucy roughness, and constrains the garb
Quite from his nature: he cannot flatter, he,—
An honest mind and plain,—he must speak truth!
An they will take it, so; if not, he's plain. 95
These kind of knaves I know, which in this plainness
Harbour more craft and more corrupter ends
Than twenty silly ducking observants
That stretch their duties nicely.

Kent. Sir, in good faith, in sincere verity, 100
Under the allowance of your great aspect,
Whose influence, like the wreath of radiant fire
On flickering Phœbus' front,—

Corn. What mean'st by this?

Kent. To go out of my dialect, which you discommend
so much. I know, sir, I am no flatterer: he that beguiled 105
you in a plain accent was a plain knave; which, for my
part, I will not be, though I should win your displeasure to
entreat me to't.

Corn. What was the offence you gave him?

Osw. I never gave him any: 110
It pleased the king his master very late
To strike at me, upon his misconstruction;
When he, conjunct, and flattering his displeasure,
Tripp'd me behind; being down, insulted, rail'd,
And put upon him such a deal of man, 115

That worthied him, got praises of the king
For him attempting who was self-subdued;
And in the fleshment of this dread exploit
Drew on me here again.
KENT. None of these rogues and cowards
But Ajax is their fool.
CORN. Fetch forth the stocks! 120
You stubborn ancient knave, you reverend braggart,
We'll teach you—
KENT. Sir, I am too old to learn:
Call not your stocks for me: I serve the king,
On whose employment I was sent to you:
You shall do small respect, show too bold malice 125
Against the grace and person of my master,
Stocking his messenger.
CORN. Fetch forth the stocks! As I have life and
honour,
There shall he sit till noon.
REG. Till noon! till night, my lord, and all night
too. 130
KENT. Why, madam, if I were your father's dog,
You should not use me so.
REG. Sir, being his knave, I will.
CORN. This is a fellow of the self-same colour
Our sister speaks of. Come, bring away the stocks!

(Stocks brought out.)

GLOU. Let me beseech your grace not to do so: 135
His fault is much, and the good king his master
Will check him for't: your purposed low correction
Is such as basest and contemned'st wretches
For pilferings and most common trespasses
Are punish'd with: the king must take it ill, 140
That he, so slightly valued in his messenger,
Should have him thus restrain'd.
CORN. I'll answer that.
REG. My sister may receive it much more worse,
To have her gentleman abused, assaulted,
For following her affairs. Put in his legs. 145

(Kent is put in the stocks.)

Come, my good lord, away. (*Exeunt all but Gloucester
and KENT.*)
GLOU. I am sorry for thee, friend; 'tis the duke's
pleasure,
Whose disposition, all the world well knows,
Will not be rubb'd nor stopp'd: I'll entreat for thee.
KENT. Pray, do not, sir: I have watch'd and travell'd
hard; 150
Some time I shall sleep out, the rest I'll whistle.
A good man's fortune may grow out at heels:
Give you good morrow!
GLOU. The duke's to blame in this; 'twill be ill taken.

(*Exit.*)

KENT. Good king, that must approve the common
saw, 155
Thou out of heaven's benediction comest
To the warm sun!
Approach, thou beacon to this under globe,
That by thy comfortable beams I may
Peruse this letter! Nothing almost sees miracles 160
But misery: I know 'tis from Cordelia,
Who hath most fortunately been inform'd
Of my obscured course; and shall find time
From this enormous state, seeking to give
Losses their remedies. All weary and o'er-watch'd,

165
Take vantage, heavy eyes, not to behold
This shameful lodging.
Fortune, good night: smile once more; turn thy
wheel!

(*Sleeps.*)

SCENE III. A WOOD

(*Enter Edgar.*)

EDG. I heard myself proclaim'd;
And by the happy hollow of a tree
Escaped the hunt. No port is free; no place,
That guard and most unusual vigilance

Does not attend my taking. Whiles I may 'scape 5
I will preserve myself: and am bethought
To take the basest and most poorest shape
That ever penury in contempt of man
Brought near to beast: my face I'll grime with filth,
Blanket my loins, elf all my hair in knots, 10
And with presented nakedness out-face
The winds and persecutions of the sky.
The country gives me proof and precedent
Of Bedlam beggars, who with roaring voices
Strike in their numb'd and mortified bare arms 15
Pins, wooden pricks, nails, sprigs of rosemary;
And with this horrible object, from low farms,
Poor pelting villages, sheep-cotes and mills,
Sometime with lunatic bans, sometime with prayers,
Enforce their charity. Poor Turlygod! poor Tom! 20
That's something yet: Edgar I nothing am. *(Exit.)*

SCENE IV. BEFORE GLOUCESTER'S CASTLE. KENT
IN THE STOCKS.

(Enter LEAR, Fool, and Gentleman.)

LEAR. 'Tis strange that they should so depart from
    home,
And not send back my messenger.
GENT. As I learn'd,
The night before there was no purpose in them
Of this remove.
KENT. Hail to thee, noble master!
LEAR. Ha! 5
Makest thou this shame thy pastime?
KENT. No, my lord.
FOOL. Ha, ha! he wears cruel garters. Horses are tied
by the heads, dogs and bears by the neck, monkeys
    by the
loins, and men by the legs. when a man's
    over-lusty at
legs, then he wears wooden nether-stocks. 10
LEAR. What's he that hath so much thy place
    mistook
To set thee here?
KENT. It is both he and she;

Your son and daughter.
LEAR. No.
KENT. Yes. 15
LEAR. No, I say.
KENT. I say, yea.
LEAR. No, no, they would not.
KENT. Yes, they have.
LEAR. By Jupiter, I swear, no. 20
KENT. By Juno, I swear, ay.
LEAR. They durst not do't;
They could not, would not do't; 'tis worse than
    murder,
To do upon respect such violent outrage:
Resolve me with all modest haste which way
Thou mightst deserve, or they impose, this usage, 25
Coming from us.
KENT. My lord, when at their home
I did commend your highness' letters to them,
Ere I was risen from the place that show'd
My duty kneeling, came there a reeking post,
Stew'd in his haste, half breathless, panting forth 30
From Goneril his mistress salutations;
Deliver'd letters, spite of intermission,
Which presently they read: on whose contents
They summon'd up their meiny, straight took horse;
Commanded me to follow and attend 35
The leisure of their answer; gave me cold looks:
And meeting here the other messenger,
Whose welcome, I perceived, had poison'd mine—
Being the very fellow that of late
Display'd so saucily against your highness— 40
Having more man than wit about me, drew:
He raised the house with loud and coward cries.
Your son and daughter found this trespass worth
The shame which here it suffers.
FOOL. Winter's not gone yet, if the wild geese fly
    that way. 45
Fathers that wear rags
Do make their children blind;
But fathers that bear bags
Shall see their children kind.
Fortune, that arrant whore, 50
Ne'er turns the key to the poor.

But, for all this, thou shalt have as many dolours
    for thy
daughters as thou canst tell in a year.
LEAR. O, how this mother swells up toward my
    heart!
Hysterica passio, down, thou climbing sorrow, 55
Thy element's below! Where is this daughter?
KENT. With the earl, sir, here within.
LEAR. Follow me not; stay here. *(Exit.)*
GENT. Made you no more offence but what you
    speak of?
KENT. None. 60
How chance the king comes with so small a train?
FOOL. An thou hadst been set i' the stocks for that
question, thou hadst well deserved it.
KENT. Why, fool?
FOOL. We'll set thee to school to an ant, to teach
    thee 65
there's no labouring i' the winter. All that follow
    their
noses are led by their eyes but blind men; and
    there's not
a nose among twenty but can smell him that's
    stinking. Let
go thy hold when a great wheel runs down a hill,
    lest it
break thy neck with following it; but the great one
    that 70
goes up the hill, let him draw thee after. When a
    wise man
gives thee better counsel, give me mine again: I
    would have
none but knaves follow it, since a fool gives it.
That sir which serves and seeks for gain,
And follows but for form, 75
Will pack when it begins to rain,
And leave thee in the storm.
But I will tarry; the fool will stay,
And let the wise man fly:
The knave turns fool that runs away; 80
The fool no knave, perdy.
KENT. Where learned you this, fool?
FOOL. Not i' the stocks, fool.

(Re-enter Lear, with Gloucester.)

Lear. Deny to speak with me? They are sick? they
    are weary?
They have travell'd all the night? Mere fetches; 85
The images of revolt and flying off.
Fetch me a better answer.
Glou. My dear lord,
You know the fiery quality of the duke;
How unremoveable and fix'd he is
In his own course. 90
Lear. Vengeance! plague! death! confusion!
Fiery? what quality? Why, Gloucester, Gloucester,
I'ld speak with the Duke of Cornwall and his wife.
Glou. Well, my good lord, I have inform'd them so.
Lear. Inform'd them! Dost thou understand me,
    man? 95
Glou. Ay, my good lord.
Lear. The king would speak with Cornwall; the dear
    father
Would with his daughter speak, commands her
    service:
Are they inform'd of this? My breath and blood!
'Fiery'? 'the fiery duke'? Tell the hot duke that— 100
No, but not yet: may be he is not well:
Infirmity doth still neglect all office
Whereto our health is bound; we are not ourselves
When nature being oppress'd commands the mind
To suffer with the body: I'll forbear; 105
And am fall'n out with my more headier will,
To take the indisposed and sickly fit
For the sound man. *(Looking on Kent)* Death on my
    state! wherefore
Should he sit here? This act persuades me
That this remotion of the duke and her 110
Is practice only. Give me my servant forth.
Go tell the duke and's wife I'ld speak with them,
Now, presently: bid them come forth and hear me,
Or at their chamber-door I'll beat the drum
Till it cry sleep to death. 115
Glou. I would have all well betwixt you. *(Exit.)*
Lear. O me, my heart, my rising heart! But down!
Fool. Cry to it, nuncle, as the cockney did to the eels

when she put 'em i' the paste alive; she knapped 'em
  o' the
coxcombs with a stick, and cried 'Down, wantons,
  down!' 120
'Twas her brother that, in pure kindness to his horse,
  buttered
his hay.

*(RE-ENTER GLOUCESTER, WITH CORNWALL, REGAN, AND
SERVANTS.)*

LEAR. Good morrow to you both.
CORN. Hail to your grace!

(Kent is set at liberty.)

REG. I am glad to see your highness.
LEAR. Regan, I think you are; I know what reason 125
I have to think so: if thou shouldst not be glad,
I would divorce me from thy mother's tomb,
Sepulchring an adultress. *(To Kent)* O, are you free?
Some other time for that. Beloved Regan,
Thy sister's naught: O Regan, she hath tied 130
Sharp-tooth'd unkindness, like a vulture, here:

(Points to his heart.)

I can scarce speak to thee; thou'lt not believe
With how depraved a quality—O Regan!
REG. I pray you, sir, take patience: I have hope
You less know how to value her desert 135
Than she to scant her duty.
LEAR. Say, how is that?
REG. I cannot think my sister in the least
Would fail her obligation: if, sir, perchance
She have restrain'd the riots of your followers,
'Tis on such ground and to such wholesome end 140
As clears her from all blame.
LEAR. My curses on her!
REG. O, sir, you are old;
Nature in you stands on the very verge
Of her confine: you should be ruled and led
By some discretion that discerns your state 145

Better than you yourself. Therefore I pray you
That to our sister you do make return;
Say you have wrong'd her, sir.
LEAR. Ask her forgiveness?
Do you but mark how this becomes the house:
(Kneeling) 'Dear daughter, I confess that I am old; [150]
Age is unnecessary: on my knees I beg
That you'll vouchsafe me raiment, bed and food.'
REG. Good sir, no more; these are unsightly tricks:
Return you to my sister.
LEAR. *(Rising)* Never, Regan:
She hath abated me of half my train; [155]
Look'd black upon me; struck me with her tongue,
Most serpent-like, upon the very heart:
All the stored vengeances of heaven fall
On her ingrateful top! Strike her young bones,
You taking airs, with lameness.
CORN. Fie, sir, fie! [160]
LEAR. You nimble lightnings, dart your blinding
      flames
Into her scornful eyes. Infect her beauty,
You fen-suck'd fogs, drawn by the powerful sun
To fall and blast her pride.
REG. O the blest gods! so will you wish on me, [165]
When the rash mood is on.
LEAR. No, Regan, thou shalt never have my curse:
Thy tender-hefted nature shall not give
Thee o'er to harshness: her eyes are fierce, but thine
Do comfort and not burn. 'Tis not in thee [170]
To grudge my pleasures, to cut off my train,
To bandy hasty words, to scant my sizes,
And in conclusion to oppose the bolt
Against my coming in: thou better know'st
The offices of nature, bond of childhood, [175]
Effects of courtesy, dues of gratitude;
Thy half o' the kingdom hast thou not forgot,
Wherein I thee endow'd.
REG. Good sir, to the purpose.
LEAR. Who put my man i' the stocks? *(Tucket within.)*
CORN. What trumpet's that?
REG. I know't; my sister's: this approves her
      letter, [180]
That she would soon be here.

(ENTER OSWALD.)

Is your lady come?
LEAR. This is a slave whose easy-borrow'd pride
Dwells in the fickle grace of her he follows.
Out, varlet, from my sight!
CORN. What means your grace?
LEAR. Who stock'd my servant? Regan, I have good
    hope 185
Thou didst not know on't. Who comes here?

(ENTER GONERIL.)

O heavens,
If you do love old men, if your sweet sway
Allow obedience, if yourselves are old,
Make it your cause; send down, and take my part!
(To Gon.) Art not ashamed to look upon this
    beard? 190
O Regan, wilt thou take her by the hand?
GON. Why not by the hand, sir? How have I
    offended?
All's not offence that indiscretion finds
And dotage terms so.
LEAR. O sides, you are too tough;
Will you yet hold? How came my man i' the
    stocks? 195
CORN. I set him there, sir: but his own disorders
Deserved much less advancement.
LEAR. You! did you?
REG. I pray you, father, being weak, seem so.
If, till the expiration of your month,
You will return and sojourn with my sister, 200
Dismissing half your train, come then to me:
I am now from home and out of that provision
Which shall be needful for your entertainment.
LEAR. Return to her, and fifty men dismiss'd?
No, rather I abjure all roofs, and choose 205
To wage against the enmity o' the air,
To be a comrade with the wolf and owl,—
Necessity's sharp pinch! Return with her?
Why, the hot-blooded France, that dowerless took
Our youngest born, I could as well be brought 210

To knee his throne, and, squire-like, pension beg
To keep base life afoot. Return with her?
Persuade me rather to be slave and sumpter
To this detested groom. *(Pointing at Oswald.)*
GON. At your choice, sir.
LEAR. I prithee, daughter, do not make me mad: 215
I will not trouble thee, my child; farewell:
We'll no more meet, no more see one another:
But yet thou art my flesh, my blood, my daughter;
Or rather a disease that's in my flesh,
Which I must needs call mine: thou art a boil, 220
A plague-sore, an embossed carbuncle,
In my corrupted blood. But I'll not chide thee;
Let shame come when it will, I do not call it:
I do not bid the thunder-bearer shoot,
Nor tell tales of thee to high-judging Jove: 225
Mend when thou canst; be better at thy leisure:
I can be patient; I can stay with Regan,
I and my hundred knights.
REG. Not altogether so:
I look'd not for you yet, nor am provided
For your fit welcome. Give ear, sir, to my sister; 230
For those that mingle reason with your passion
Must be content to think you old, and so—
But she knows what she does.
LEAR. Is this well spoken?
REG. I dare avouch it, sir: what, fifty followers?
Is it not well? What should you need of more? 235
Yea, or so many, sith that both charge and danger
Speak 'gainst so great a number? How in one house
Should many people under two commands
Hold amity? 'Tis hard, almost impossible.
GON. Why might not you, my lord, receive
     attendance 240
From those that she calls servants or from mine?
REG. Why not, my lord? If then they chanced to
     slack you,
We could control them. If you will come to me,
For now I spy a danger, I entreat you
To bring but five and twenty: to no more 245
Will I give place or notice.
LEAR. I gave you all—
REG. And in good time you gave it.

LEAR. Made you my guardians, my depositaries,
But kept a reservation to be follow'd
With such a number. What, must I come to you 250
With five and twenty, Regan? said you so?
REG. And speak't again, my lord; no more with me.
LEAR. Those wicked creatures yet do look well-
favour'd,
When others are more wicked; not being the worst
Stands in some rank of praise. (To GON.) I'll go with
thee: 255
Thy fifty yet doth double five and twenty,
And thou art twice her love.
GON. Hear me, my lord:
What need you five and twenty, ten, or five,
To follow in a house where twice so many
Have a command to tend you?
REG. What need one? 260
LEAR. O, reason not the need: our basest beggars
Are in the poorest thing superfluous:
Allow not nature more than nature needs,
Man's life's as cheap as beast's: thou art a lady;
If only to go warm were gorgeous, 265
Why, nature needs not what thou gorgeous wear'st,
Which scarcely keeps thee warm. But for true need,
—

You heavens, give me that patience, patience I need!
You see me here, you gods, a poor old man,
As full of grief as age; wretched in both: 270
If it be you that stirs these daughters' hearts
Against their father, fool me not so much
To bear it tamely; touch me with noble anger,
And let not women's weapons, water-drops,
Stain my man's cheeks! No, you unnatural hags, 275
I will have such revenges on you both
That all the world shall—I will do such things,—
What they are, yet I know not, but they shall be
The terrors of the earth. You think I'll weep;
No, I'll not weep: 280
I have full cause of weeping; but this heart
Shall break into a hundred thousand flaws,
Or ere I'll weep. O fool, I shall go mad!

(Exeunt Lear, Gloucester, Kent, and Fool.)

CORN. Let us withdraw; 'twill be a storm.

(Storm and tempest.)

REG. This house is little: the old man and his
    people 285
Cannot be well bestow'd.
GON. 'Tis his own blame; hath put himself from rest,
And must needs taste his folly.
REG. For his particular, I'll receive him gladly,
But not one follower.
GON. So am I purposed. 290
Where is my lord of Gloucester?
CORN. Follow'd the old man forth: he is return'd.

(RE-ENTER GLOUCESTER.)

GLOU. The king is in high rage.
CORN. Whither is he going?
GLOU. He calls to horse; but will I know not whither.
CORN. 'Tis best to give him way; he leads himself. 295
GON. My lord, entreat him by no means to stay.
GLOU. Alack, the night comes on, and the bleak
    winds
Do sorely ruffle; for many miles about
There's scarce a bush.
REG. O, sir, to wilful men
The injuries that they themselves procure 300
Must be their schoolmasters. Shut up your doors:
He is attended with a desperate train;
And what they may incense him to, being apt
To have his ear abused, wisdom bids fear.
CORN. Shut up your doors, my lord; 'tis a wild
    night: 305
My Regan counsels well: come out o' the storm.
    (Exeunt.)

ACT III.

(Storm still. Enter KENT and a Gentleman, meeting.)

KENT. Who's there, besides foul weather?
GENT. One minded like the weather, most unquietly.
KENT. I know you. Where's the king?
GENT. Contending with the fretful elements;
Bids the wind blow the earth into the sea, 5
Or swell the curled waters 'bove the main,
That things might change or cease; tears his white hair,
Which the impetuous blasts, with eyeless rage,
Catch in their fury, and make nothing of;
Strives in his little world of man to out-scorn 10
The to-and-fro-conflicting wind and rain.
This night, wherein the cub-drawn bear would couch,
The lion and the belly-pinched wolf
Keep their fur dry, unbonneted he runs,
And bids what will take all. 15
KENT. But who is with him?
GENT. None but the fool; who labours to out-jest
His heart-struck injuries.
KENT. Sir, I do know you;
And dare, upon the warrant of my note,
Commend a dear thing to you. There is division,

Although as yet the face of it be cover'd 20
With mutual cunning, 'twixt Albany and Cornwall;
Who have—as who have not, that their great stars
Throned and set high?—servants, who seem no less,
Which are to France the spies and speculations
Intelligent of our state; what hath been seen, 25
Either in snuffs and packings of the dukes,
Or the hard rein which both of them have borne
Against the old kind king, or something deeper,
Whereof perchance these are but furnishings,—
But true it is, from France there comes a power 30
Into this scatter'd kingdom; who already,
Wise in our negligence, have secret feet
In some of our best ports, and are at point
To show their open banner. Now to you:
If on my credit you dare build so far 35
To make your speed to Dover, you shall find
Some that will thank you, making just report
Of how unnatural and bemadding sorrow
The king hath cause to plain.
I am a gentleman of blood and breeding, 40
And from some knowledge and assurance offer
This office to you.
Gent. I will talk further with you.
Kent. No, do not.
For confirmation that I am much more
Than my out-wall, open this purse and take 45
What it contains. If you shall see Cordelia,—
As fear not but you shall,—show her this ring,
And she will tell you who your fellow is
That yet you do not know. Fie on this storm!
I will go seek the king.
Gent. Give me your hand: 50
Have you no more to say?
Kent. Few words, but, to effect, more than all yet;
That when we have found the king,—in which
    your pain
That way, I'll this,—he that first lights on him
Holla the other. *(Exeunt severally.)* 55

SCENE II. ANOTHER PART OF THE HEATH. STORM STILL.

(Enter LEAR and Fool.)

LEAR. Blow, winds, and crack your cheeks! rage! blow!
You cataracts and hurricanoes, spout
Till you have drench'd our steeples, drown'd the cocks!
You sulphurous and thought-executing fires,
Vaunt-couriers to oak-cleaving thunderbolts, 5
Singe my white head! And thou, all-shaking thunder,
Smite flat the thick rotundity o' the world!
Crack nature's moulds, all germins spill at once
That make ingrateful man!
FOOL. O nuncle, court holy-water in a dry house is 10
better than this rain-water out o' door. Good nuncle, in,
and ask thy daughters' blessing: here's a night pities neither
wise man nor fool.
LEAR. Rumble thy bellyful! Spit, fire! spout, rain!
Nor rain, wind, thunder, fire, are my daughters: 15
I tax not you, you elements, with unkindness;
I never gave you kingdom, call'd you children,
You owe me no subscription: then let fall
Your horrible pleasure; here I stand, your slave,
A poor, infirm, weak and despised old man: 20
But yet I call you servile ministers,
That have with two pernicious daughters join'd
Your high-engender'd battles 'gainst a head
So old and white as this. O! O! 'tis foul!
FOOL. He that has a house to put's head in has a good 25
head-piece.
The cod-piece that will house
Before the head has any,
The head and he shall louse;
So beggars marry many. 30
The man that makes his toe
What he his heart should make

Shall of a corn cry woe,
And turn his sleep to wake.
For there was never yet fair woman but she made
    mouths 35
in a glass.
Lear. No, I will be the pattern of all patience;
I will say nothing.

(Enter Kent.)

Kent. Who's there?
Fool. Marry, here's grace and a cod-piece; that's a 40
wise man and a fool.
Kent. Alas, sir, are you here? things that love night
Love not such nights as these; the wrathful skies
Gallow the very wanderers of the dark,
And make them keep their caves: since I was man, 45
Such sheets of fire, such bursts of horrid thunder,
Such groans of roaring wind and rain, I never
Remember to have heard: man's nature cannot carry
The affliction nor the fear.
Lear. Let the great gods,
That keep this dreadful pother o'er our heads, 50
Find out their enemies now. Tremble, thou wretch,
That hast within thee undivulged crimes,
Unwhipp'd of justice: hide thee, thou bloody hand;
Thou perjured, and thou simular man of virtue
That art incestuous: caitiff, to pieces shake, 55
That under covert and convenient seeming
Hast practised on man's life: close pent-up guilts,
Rive your concealing continents and cry
These dreadful summoners grace. I am a man
More sinn'd against than sinning.
Kent. Alack, bare-headed! 60
Gracious my lord, hard by here is a hovel;
Some friendship will it lend you 'gainst the tempest:
Repose you there; while I to this hard house—
More harder than the stones whereof 'tis raised;
Which even but now, demanding after you, 65
Denied me to come in—return, and force
Their scanted courtesy.
Lear. My wits begin to turn.
Come on, my boy: how dost, my boy? art cold?

I am cold myself. Where is this straw, my fellow?
The art of our necessities is strange, 70
That can make vile things precious. Come, your
    hovel.
Poor fool and knave, I have one part in my heart
That's sorry yet for thee.

FOOL. *(Singing)* He that has and a little tiny wit,—
With hey, ho, the wind and the rain,— 75
Must make content with his fortunes fit,
For the rain it raineth every day.

LEAR. True, my good boy. Come, bring us to this
    hovel. *(Exeunt Lear and KENT.)*

FOOL. This is a brave night to cool a courtezan.
    I'll
speak a prophecy ere I go: 80
When priests are more in word than matter;
When brewers mar their malt with water;
When nobles are their tailors' tutors;
No heretics burn'd, but wenches' suitors;
When every case in law is right; 85
No squire in debt, nor no poor knight;
When slanders do not live in tongues,
Nor cutpurses come not to throngs;
When usurers tell their gold i' the field,
And bawds and whores do churches build; 90
Then shall the realm of Albion
Come to great confusion:
Then comes the time, who lives to see't,
That going shall be used with feet.
This prophecy Merlin shall make; for I live before his
    time. 95
(Exit.)

SCENE III. GLOUCESTER'S CASTLE

(Enter Gloucester and Edmund.)

GLOU. Alack, alack, Edmund, I like not this
    unnatural
dealing. When I desired their leave that I might
    pity him,
they took from me the use of mine own house;
    charged

me, on pain of their perpetual displeasure, neither to
    speak
of him, entreat for him, nor any way sustain him. ₅
EDM. Most savage and unnatural!
GLOU. Go to; say you nothing. There's a division
    betwixt
the dukes, and a worse matter than that: I have
    received
a letter this night; 'tis dangerous to be spoken; I
have locked the letter in my closet: these injuries the
    king ₁₀
now bears will be revenged home; there is part of a
    power
already footed: we must incline to the king. I
    will seek
him and privily relieve him: go you, and maintain
    talk
with the duke, that my charity be not of him
    perceived: if
he ask for me, I am ill and gone to bed. Though I
    die ₁₅
for it, as no less is threatened me, the king my old
    master
must be relieved. There is some strange thing
    toward,
Edmund; pray you, be careful. *(Exit.)*
EDM. This courtesy, forbid thee, shall the duke
Instantly know, and of that letter too: ₂₀
This seems a fair deserving, and must draw me
That which my father loses; no less than all:
The younger rises when the old doth fall. *(Exit.)*

SCENE IV. THE HEATH. BEFORE A HOVEL

(Enter Lear, Kent, and Fool.)

KENT. Here is the place, my lord; good my lord,
    enter:
The tyranny of the open night's too rough
For nature to endure. *(Storm still.)*
LEAR. Let me alone.
KENT. Good my lord, enter here.
LEAR. Wilt break my heart?

KENT. I had rather break mine own. Good my lord,
    enter. 5
LEAR. Thou think'st 'tis much that this contentious
    storm
Invades us to the skin: so 'tis to thee;
But where the greater malady is fix'd
The lesser is scarce felt. Thou'ldst shun a bear,
But if thy flight lay toward the raging sea 10
Thou'ldst meet the bear i' the mouth. When the
    mind's free
The body's delicate: the tempest in my mind
Doth from my senses take all feeling else
Save what beats there. Filial ingratitude!
Is it not as this mouth should tear this hand 15
For lifting food to't? But I will punish home
No, I will weep no more. In such a night
To shut me out! Pour on; I will endure.
In such a night as this! O Regan, Goneril!
Your old kind father, whose frank heart gave you
    all,— 20
O, that way madness lies; let me shun that;
No more of that.
KENT. Good my lord, enter here.
LEAR. Prithee, go in thyself; seek thine own ease:
This tempest will not give me leave to ponder
On things would hurt me more. But I'll go in. 25
(To the Fool) In, boy; go first. You houseless poverty,—

Nay, get thee in. I'll pray, and then I'll sleep.

(Fool goes in.)

Poor naked wretches, wheresoe'er you are,
That bide the pelting of this pitiless storm,
How shall your houseless heads and unfed sides, 30
Your loop'd and window'd raggedness, defend you
From seasons such as these? O, I have ta'en
Too little care of this! Take physic, pomp;
Expose thyself to feel what wretches feel,
That thou mayst shake the superflux to them 35
And show the heavens more just.
EDG. *(Within)* Fathom and half, fathom and half!
Poor Tom! *(The Fool runs out from the hovel.)*

FOOL. Come not in here, nuncle, here's a spirit. Help
me, help me! 40

KENT. Give me thy hand. Who's there?

FOOL. A spirit, a spirit: he says his name's poor Tom.

KENT. What art thou that dost grumble there i' the
straw?
Come forth.

(Enter EDGAR disguised as a madman.)

EDG. Away! the foul fiend follows me! 'Through
the 45
sharp hawthorn blows the cold wind.' Hum! go
to thy
cold bed and warm thee.

LEAR. Hast thou given all to thy two daughters? and
art thou come to this?

EDG. Who gives any thing to poor Tom? whom the 50
foul fiend hath led through fire and through flame,
through
ford and whirlpool, o'er bog and quagmire; that
hath laid
knives under his pillow and halters in his pew; set
ratsbane
by his porridge; made him proud of heart, to
ride on
a bay trotting-horse over four-inched bridges, to
course his 55
own shadow for a traitor. Bless thy five wits! Tom's
a-cold. O, do de, do de, do de. Bless thee from
whirlwinds,
star-blasting, and taking! Do poor Tom some
charity, whom the foul fiend vexes. There could I
have him
now, and there, and there again, and there. *(Storm
still.)* 60

LEAR. What, have his daughters brought him to this
pass?
Couldst thou save nothing? Didst thou give
them all?

FOOL. Nay, he reserved a blanket, else we had
been all
shamed.

LEAR. Now, all the plagues that in the pendulous air $_{65}$
Hang fated o'er men's faults light on thy daughters!
KENT. He hath no daughters, sir.
LEAR. Death, traitor! nothing could have subdued nature
To such a lowness but his unkind daughters.
Is it the fashion that discarded fathers $_{70}$
Should have thus little mercy on their flesh?
Judicious punishment! 'twas this flesh begot
Those pelican daughters.
EDG. Pillicock sat on Pillicock-hill:
Halloo, halloo, loo, loo! $_{75}$
FOOL. This cold night will turn us all to fools and madmen
EDG. Take heed o' the foul fiend: obey thy parents;
keep thy word justly; swear not; commit not with man's
sworn spouse; set not thy sweet heart on proud array. $_{80}$
Tom's a-cold.
LEAR. What hast thou been?
EDG. A serving-man, proud in heart and mind; that
curled my hair; wore gloves in my cap; served the lust of
my mistress' heart and did the act of darkness with her; $_{85}$
swore as many oaths as I spake words and broke them in
the sweet face of heaven: one that slept in the contriving of
lust and waked to do it: wine loved I deeply, dice dearly,
and in woman out-paramoured the Turk: false of heart,
light of ear, bloody of hand; hog in sloth, fox in stealth, $_{90}$
wolf in greediness, dog in madness, lion in prey. Let not
the creaking of shoes nor the rustling of silks betray thy
poor heart to woman: keep thy foot out of brothels, thy

hand out of plackets, thy pen from lenders' books, and defy
the foul fiend. 95
'Still through the hawthorn blows the cold wind.'
Says suum, mun, ha, no, nonny.
Dolphin my boy, my boy, sessa! let him trot by.

(Storm still.)

LEAR. Why, thou wert better in thy grave than to answer
with thy uncovered body this extremity of the skies. 100
Is man no more than this? Consider him well. Thou owest
the worm no silk, the beast no hide, the sheep no wool, the
cat no perfume. Ha! here's three on's are sophisticated.
Thou art the thing itself: unaccommodated man is no more
but such a poor, bare, forked animal as thou art. Off, off, 105
you lendings! come, unbutton here.

(Tearing off his clothes.)

FOOL. Prithee, nuncle, be contented; 'tis a naughty night
to swim in. Now a little fire in a wild field were like an
old lecher's heart, a small spark, all the rest on's body cold.
Look, here comes a walking fire. 110

Enter GLOUCESTER, with a torch.

EDG. This is the foul fiend Flibbertigibbet: he begins at
curfew and walks till the first cock; he gives the web and
the pin, squints the eye and makes the hare-lip; mildews

the white wheat and hurts the poor creature of earth.
Saint Withold footed thrice the 'old; 115
He met the night-mare and her nine-fold;
Bid her alight,
And her troth plight,
And aroint thee, witch, aroint thee!
KENT. How fares your grace? 120
LEAR. What's he?
KENT. Who's there? What is't you seek?
GLOU. What are you there? Your names?
EDG. Poor Tom, that eats the swimming frog, the
      toad,
the tadpole, the wall-newt and the water; that in the
      fury 125
of his heart, when the foul fiend rages, eats
      cow-dung for
sallets; swallows the old rat and the ditch-dog;
      drinks the
green mantle of the standing pool; who is whipped
      from
tithing to tithing, and stock-punished, and
      imprisoned;
who hath had three suits to his back, six shirts to his
      body, 130
horse to ride and weapon to wear;
But mice and rats and such small deer
Have been Tom's food for seven long year.
Beware my follower. Peace, Smulkin, peace, thou
      fiend!
GLOU. What, hath your grace no better company? 135
EDG. The prince of darkness is a gentleman: Modo
he's call'd, and Mahu.
GLOU. Our flesh and blood is grown so vile, my lord,
That it doth hate what gets it.
EDG. Poor Tom's a-cold. 140
GLOU. Go in with me: my duty cannot suffer
To obey in all your daughters' hard commands:
Though their injunction be to bar my doors
And let this tyrannous night take hold upon you,
Yet have I ventured to come seek you out 145
And bring you where both fire and food is ready.
LEAR. First let me talk with this philosopher.
What is the cause of thunder?

KENT. Good my lord, take his offer; go into the
    house.
LEAR. I'll talk a word with this same learned
    Theban. 150
What is your study?
EDG. How to prevent the fiend and to kill vermin.
LEAR. Let me ask you one word in private.
KENT. Importune him once more to go, my lord;
His wits begin to unsettle.
GLOU. Canst thou blame him? *(Storm still.)* 155
His daughters seek his death: ah, that good Kent!
He said it would be thus, poor banish'd man!
Thou say'st the king grows mad; I'll tell thee, friend,
I am almost mad myself: I had a son,
Now outlaw'd from my blood; he sought my life, 160
But lately, very late: I loved him, friend,
No father his son dearer: truth to tell thee,
The grief hath crazed my wits. What a night's this!
I do beseech your grace,—
LEAR. O, cry you mercy, sir.
Noble philosopher, your company. 165
EDG. Tom's a-cold.
GLOU. In, fellow, there, into the hovel: keep thee
    warm.
LEAR. Come, let's in all.
KENT. This way, my lord.
LEAR. With him;
I will keep still with my philosopher.
KENT. Good my lord, soothe him; let him take the
    fellow. 170
GLOU. Take him you on.
KENT. Sirrah, come on; go along with us.
LEAR. Come, good Athenian.
GLOU. No words, no words: hush.
EDG. Child Rowland to the dark tower came: 175
His word was still 'Fie, foh, and fum,
I smell the blood of a British man.' *(Exeunt.)*

SCENE V. GLOUCESTER'S CASTLE

(Enter Cornwall and Edmund.)

CORN. I will have my revenge ere I depart his house.

EDM. How, my lord, I may be censured, that nature
thus gives way to loyalty, something fears me to
   think of.
CORN. I now perceive, it was not altogether your
   brother's
evil disposition made him seek his death, but a
   provoking ₅
merit, set a-work by a reproveable badness in
   himself.
EDM. How malicious is my fortune, that I must
   repent
to be just! This is the letter he spoke of, which
   approves
him an intelligent party to the advantages of
   FRANCE, O
heavens! that this treason were not, or not I the
   detector! ₁₀
CORN. Go with me to the duchess.
EDM. If the matter of this paper be certain, you have
mighty business in hand.
CORN. True or false, it hath made thee earl of
   Gloucester.
Seek out where thy father is, that he may be ready
   for our ₁₅
apprehension.
EDM. (Aside) If I find him comforting the king, it will
stuff his suspicion more fully.—I will persever in my
   course
of loyalty, though the conflict be sore between that
   and my
blood. ₂₀
CORN. I will lay trust upon thee, and thou shalt
   find a
dearer father in my love. (Exeunt.)

SCENE VI. A CHAMBER IN A FARMHOUSE ADJOINING THE CASTLE.

(ENTER GLOUCESTER, LEAR, KENT, FOOL, AND EDGAR.)

GLOU. Here is better than the open air; take it
   thankfully.
I will piece out the comfort with what addition I

can: I will not be long from you.

KENT. All the power of his wits have given way
    to his

impatience: the gods reward your kindness! 5

(Exit Gloucester.)

EDG. Fraterretto calls me, and tells me Nero is an

angler in the lake of darkness. Pray, innocent, and
    beware

the foul fiend.

FOOL. Prithee, nuncle, tell me whether a madman
    be a

gentleman or a yeoman. 10

LEAR. A king, a king!

FOOL. No, he's a yeoman that has a gentleman to his

son, for he's a mad yeoman that sees his son a
    gentleman

before him.

LEAR. To have a thousand with red burning spits 15

Come hissing in upon 'em,—

EDG. The foul fiend bites my back.

FOOL. He's mad that trusts in the tameness of a wolf,

a horse's health, a boy's love, or a whore's oath.

LEAR. It shall be done; I will arraign them straight. 20

(To Edgar) Come, sit thou here, most learned justicer;

(To the Fool) Thou, sapient sir, sit here. Now, you she
    foxes!

EDG. Look, where he stands and glares! Wantest

thou eyes at trial, madam?

Come o'er the bourn, Bessy, to me. 25

FOOL. Her boat hath a leak,

And she must not speak

Why she dares not come over to thee.

EDG. The foul fiend haunts poor Tom in the
    voice of

a nightingale. Hopdance cries in Tom's belly for two
    white 30

herring. Croak not, black angel; I have no food for
    thee.

KENT. How do you, sir? Stand you not so amazed:

Will you lie down and rest upon the cushions?

LEAR. I'll see their trial first. Bring in the evidence.

(To Edgar) Thou robed man of justice take thy
    place; 35
(To the Fool) And thou, his yoke-fellow of equity,
Bench by his side. *(To Kent)* You are o' the
    commission;
Sit you too.

EDG. Let us deal justly.
Sleepest or wakest thou, jolly shepherd? 40
Thy sheep be in the corn;
And for one blast of thy minikin mouth,
Thy sheep shall take no harm.
Pur! the cat is gray.

LEAR. Arraign her first; 'tis Goneril. I here take my 45
oath before this honourable assembly, she kicked
    the poor
king her father.

FOOL. Come hither, mistress. Is your name Goneril?

LEAR. She cannot deny it.

FOOL. Cry you mercy, I took you for a joint-stool. 50

LEAR. And here's another, whose warp'd looks
    proclaim
What store her heart is made on. Stop her there!
Arms, arms, sword, fire! Corruption in the place!
False justicer, why hast thou let her 'scape?

EDG. Bless thy five wits! 55

KENT. O pity! Sir, where is the patience now,
That you so oft have boasted to retain?

EDG. *(Aside)* My tears begin to take his part so much,
They'll mar my counterfeiting.

LEAR. The little dogs and all, 60
Tray, Blanch, and Sweet-heart, see, they bark at me.

EDG. Tom will throw his head at them. Avaunt, you
curs!
Be thy mouth or black or white,
Tooth that poisons if it bite; 65
Mastiff, greyhound, mongrel grim,
Hound or spaniel, brach or lym,
Or bobtail tike or trundle-tail,
Tom will make them weep and wail:
For, with throwing thus my head, 70
Dogs leap the hatch, and all are fled.
Do de, de, de. Sessa! Come, march to wakes and fairs
and market-towns. Poor Tom, thy horn is dry.

LEAR. Then let them anatomize Regan; see what
breeds about her heart. Is there any cause in nature
   that 75
makes these hard hearts? *(To Edgar)* You, sir, I
   entertain
for one of my hundred; only I do not like the fashion
of your garments. You will say they are Persian
   attire;
but let them be changed.

KENT. Now, good my lord, lie here and rest awhile. 80

LEAR. Make no noise, make no noise; draw the
   curtains:
so, so, so. We'll go to supper i' the morning. So,
so, so.

FOOL. And I'll go to bed at noon.

(RE-ENTER GLOUCESTER.)

GLOU. Come hither, friend: where is the king my
   master? 85

KENT. Here, sir; but trouble him not: his wits are
   gone.

GLOU. Good friend, I prithee, take him in thy arms;
I have o'erheard a plot of death upon him:
There is a litter ready; lay him in't,
And drive toward Dover, friend, where thou shalt
   meet 90
Both welcome and protection. Take up thy master:
If thou shouldst dally half an hour, his life,
With thine and all that offer to defend him,
Stand in assured loss. Take up, take up,
And follow me, that will to some provision 95
Give thee quick conduct.

KENT. Oppressed nature sleeps.
This rest might yet have balm'd thy broken sinews,
Which, if convenience will not allow,
Stand in hard cure. *(To the Fool)* Come, help to bear
   thy master;
Thou must not stay behind.

GLOU. Come, come, away. 100

(Exeunt all but Edgar.)

EDG. When we our betters see bearing our woes,
We scarcely think our miseries our foes.
Who alone suffers suffers most i' the mind,
Leaving free things and happy shows behind:
But then the mind much sufferance doth o'erskip, 105
When grief hath mates, and bearing fellowship.
How light and portable my pain seems now,
When that which makes me bend makes the
        king bow,
He childed as I father'd! Tom, away!
Mark the high noises, and thyself bewray 110
When false opinion, whose wrong thought defiles
        thee,
In thy just proof repeals and reconciles thee.
What will hap more to-night, safe 'scape the king!
Lurk, lurk. (Exit.)

SCENE VII. GLOUCESTER'S CASTLE

(Enter Cornwall, Regan, Goneril, Edmund, and Servants.)

CORN. Post speedily to my lord your husband; show
him this letter: the army of France is landed. Seek
        out the
traitor Gloucester. (Exeunt some of the Servants.)
REG. Hang him instantly.
GON. Pluck out his eyes. 5
CORN. Leave him to my displeasure. Edmund, keep
you our sister company: the revenges we are bound
        to take
upon your traitorous father are not fit for your
        beholding.
Advise the duke, where you are going, to a most
        festinate
preparation: we are bound to the like. Our posts
        shall be 10
swift and intelligent betwixt us. Farewell, dear sister;
farewell, my lord of Gloucester.

(ENTER OSWALD.)

How now! where's the king?

Osw. My lord of Gloucester hath convey'd him
    hence:
Some five or six and thirty of his knights, 15
Hot questrists after him, met him at gate;
Who, with some other of the lords dependants,
Are gone with him toward Dover; where they boast
To have well-armed friends.
Corn. Get horses for your mistress.
Gon. Farewell, sweet lord, and sister. 20
Corn. Edmund, farewell.

          (Exeunt Goneril, Edmund, and Oswald.)

Go seek the traitor Gloucester.
Pinion him like a thief, bring him before us.

          (Exeunt other Servants.)

Though well we may not pass upon his life
Without the form of justice, yet our power
Shall do a courtesy to our wrath, which men 25
May blame but not control. Who's there? the traitor?

    (Enter GLOUCESTER, brought in by two or three.)

Reg. Ingrateful fox! 'tis he.
Corn. Bind fast his corky arms.
Glou. What mean your graces? Good my friends,
    consider
You are my guests: do me no foul play, friends. 30
Corn. Bind him, I say. (Servants bind him.)
Reg. Hard, hard. O filthy traitor!
Glou. Unmerciful lady as you are, I'm none.
Corn. To this chair bind him. Villain, thou shalt
    find—

          (Regan plucks his beard.)

Glou. By the kind gods, 'tis most ignobly done
To pluck me by the beard. 35
Reg. So white, and such a traitor!
Glou. Naughty lady,
These hairs which thou dost ravish from my chin

Will quicken and accuse thee: I am your host:
With robbers' hands my hospitable favours
You should not ruffle thus. What will you do? 40
CORN. Come, sir, what letters had you late from
    France?
REG. Be simple answerer, for we know the truth.
CORN. And what confederacy have you with the
    traitors
Late footed in the kingdom?
REG. To whose hands have you sent the lunatic
    king? 45
Speak.
GLOU. I have a letter guessingly set down,
Which came from one that's of a neutral heart
And not from one opposed.
CORN. Cunning.
REG. And false.
CORN. Where hast thou sent the king?
GLOU. To Dover. 50
REG. Wherefore to Dover? Wast thou not charged at
    peril—
CORN. Wherefore to Dover? Let him first answer
    that.
GLOU. I am tied to the stake, and I must stand the
    course.
REG. Wherefore to Dover, sir?
GLOU. Because I would not see thy cruel nails 55
Pluck out his poor old eyes, nor thy fierce sister
In his anointed flesh stick boarish fangs.
The sea, with such a storm as his bare head
In hell-black night endured, would have buoy'd up,
And quench'd the stelled fires: 60
Yet, poor old heart, he holp the heavens to rain.
If wolves had at thy gate howl'd that stern time,
Thou shouldst have said, 'Good porter, turn the key,'
All cruels else subscribed: but I shall see
The winged vengeance overtake such children. 65
CORN. See't shalt thou never. Fellows, hold the chair.
Upon these eyes of thine I'll set my foot.
GLOU. He that will think to live till he be old,
Give me some help! O cruel! O you gods!
REG. One side will mock another; the other too. 70
CORN. If you see vengeance—

First Serv. Hold your hand, my lord:
I have served you ever since I was a child;
But better service have I never done you
Than now to bid you hold.
Reg. How now, you dog!
First Serv. If you did wear a beard upon your
chin, 75
I'ld shake it on this quarrel. What do you mean?
Corn. My villain! *(They draw and fight.)*
First Serv. Nay, then, come on, and take the chance
of anger.
Reg. Give me thy sword. A peasant stand up thus!

(Takes a sword and runs at him behind.)

First Serv. O, I am slain! My lord, you have one eye
left 80
To see some mischief on him. O! *(Dies.)*
Corn. Lest it see more, prevent it. Out, vile jelly!
Where is thy lustre now?
Glou. All dark and comfortless. Where's my son
Edmund?
Edmund, enkindle all the sparks of nature, 85
To quit this horrid act.
Reg. Out, treacherous villain!
Thou call'st on him that hates thee: it was he
That made the overture of thy treasons to us;
Who is too good to pity thee.
Glou. O my follies! Then Edgar was abused. 90
Kind gods, forgive me that, and prosper him!
Reg. Go thrust him out at gates, and let him smell
His way to Dover. *(Exit one with Gloucester.)* How is't,
my lord? how look you?
Corn. I have received a hurt: follow me, lady.
Turn out that eyeless villain: throw this slave 95
Upon the dunghill. Regan, I bleed apace:
Untimely comes this hurt: give me your arm.
Sec. Serv. I'll never care what wickedness I do,
If this man come to good.
Third Serv. If she live long,
And in the end meet the old course of death, 100
Women will all turn monsters.

Sec. Serv. Let's follow the old earl, and get the
    Bedlam
To lead him where he would: his roguish madness
Allows itself to any thing.
Third Serv. Go thou: I'll fetch some flax and whites
    of eggs 105
To apply to his bleeding face. Now, heaven help him!

(Exeunt severally.)

ACT IV.

(Enter EDGAR.)

EDG. Yet better thus, and known to be contemn'd,
Than still contemn'd and flatter'd. To be worst,
The lowest and most dejected thing of fortune,
Stands still in esperance, lives not in fear:
The lamentable change is from the best; 5
The worst returns to laughter. Welcome then,
Thou unsubstantial air that I embrace!
The wretch that them hast blown unto the worst
Owes nothing to thy blasts. But who comes here?

(Enter GLOUCESTER, led by an Old Man.)

My father, poorly led? World, world, O world! 10
But that thy strange mutations make us hate thee,
Life would not yield to age.
OLD MAN. O, my good lord, I have been your tenant,
and your father's tenant, these fourscore years.
GLOU. Away, get thee away; good friend, be gone: 15
Thy comforts can do me no good at all;
Thee they may hurt.
OLD MAN. Alack, sir, you cannot see your way.
GLOU. I have no way and therefore want no eyes;

I stumbled when I saw: full oft 'tis seen, 20
Our means secure us, and our mere defects
Prove our commodities. Ah, dear son Edgar,
The food of thy abused father's wrath!
Might I but live to see thee in my touch,
I'ld say I had eyes again!
OLD MAN. How now! Who 's there? 25
EDG. (Aside) O gods! Who is't can say 'I am at the
    worst'?
I am worse than e'er I was.
OLD MAN. 'Tis poor mad Tom.
EDG. (Aside) And worse I may be yet: the worst is not
So long as we can say 'This is the worst.'
OLD MAN. Fellow, where goest?
GLOU. Is it a beggar-man? 30
OLD MAN. Madman and beggar too.
GLOU. He has some reason, else he could not beg.
I' the last night's storm I such a fellow saw,
Which made me think a man a worm: my son
Came then into my mind, and yet my mind 35
Was then scarce friends with him: I have heard more
    since.
As flies to wanton boys, are we to the gods;
They kill us for their sport.
EDG. (Aside) How should this be?
Bad is the trade that must play fool to sorrow,
Angering itself and others. Bless thee, master! 40
GLOU. Is that the naked fellow?
OLD MAN. Ay, my lord.
GLOU. Then, prithee, get thee gone: if for my sake
Thou wilt o'ertake us hence a mile or twain
I' the way toward Dover, do it for ancient love;
And bring some covering for this naked soul, 45
Who I'll entreat to lead me.
OLD MAN. Alack, sir, he is mad.
GLOU. 'Tis the times' plague, when madmen lead the
    blind.
Do as I bid thee, or rather do thy pleasure;
Above the rest, be gone.
OLD MAN. I'll bring him the best 'parel that I have, 50
Come on't what will. *(Exit.)*
GLOU. Sirrah, naked fellow,—

EDG. Poor Tom's a-cold. *(Aside)* I cannot daub it
  further.
GLOU. Come hither, fellow.
EDG. (Aside) And yet I must. Bless thy sweet eyes,
  they bleed. 55
GLOU. Know'st thou the way to Dover?
EDG. Both stile and gate, horse-way and
  foot-path. Poor
Tom hath been scared out of his good wits. Bless
  thee, good
man's son, from the foul fiend! Five fiends have been
  in poor
Tom at once; of lust, as Obidicut; Hobbididence,
  prince of 60
dumbness; Mahu, of stealing; Modo, of murder;
  Flibbertigibbet,
of mopping and mowing; who since possesses
chambermaids and waiting-women. So, bless thee,
  master!
GLOU. Here, take this purse, thou whom the
  heavens' plagues
Have humbled to all strokes: that I am wretched 65
Makes thee the happier. Heavens, deal so still!
Let the superfluous and lust-dieted man,
That slaves your ordinance, that will not see
Because he doth not feel, feel your power quickly;
So distribution should undo excess 70
And each man have enough. Dost thou know
  Dover?
EDG. Ay, master.
GLOU. There is a cliff whose high and bending head
Looks fearfully in the confined deep:
Bring me but to the very brim of it, 75
And I'll repair the misery thou dost bear
With something rich about me: from that place
I shall no leading need.
EDG. Give me thy arm:
Poor Tom shall lead thee. *(Exeunt.)*

SCENE II. BEFORE THE DUKE OF ALBANY'S PALACE.

(ENTER GONERIL AND EDMUND.)

Gon. Welcome, my lord: I marvel our mild husband
Not met us on the way.

(ENTER OSWALD.)

Now, where's your master?
Osw. Madam, within; but never man so changed.
I told him of the army that was landed;
He smiled at it: I told him you were coming; 5
His answer was, 'The worse:' of Gloucester's
    treachery
And of the loyal service of his son
When I inform'd him, then he call'd me sot
And told me I had turn'd the wrong side out:
What most he should dislike seems pleasant to
    him; 10
What like, offensive.
Gon. *(To Edm.)* Then shall you go no further.
It is the cowish terror of his spirit,
That dares not undertake: he'll not feel wrongs,
Which tie him to an answer. Our wishes on the way
May prove effects. Back, Edmund, to my brother; 15
Hasten his musters and conduct his powers:
I must change arms at home and give the distaff
Into my husband's hands. This trusty servant
Shall pass between us: ere long you are like to hear,
If you dare venture in your own behalf, 20
A mistress's command. Wear this; spare speech;

(Giving a favour.)

Decline your head: this kiss, if it durst speak,
Would stretch thy spirits up into the air:
Conceive, and fare thee well.
Edm. Yours in the ranks of death.
Gon. My most dear Gloucester! 25

(Exit Edmund.)

O, the difference of man and man!
To thee a woman's services are due:
My fool usurps my body.
Osw. Madam, here comes my lord. *(Exit.)*

(ENTER ALBANY.)

Gon. I have been worth the whistle.
Alb. O Goneril!
You are not worth the dust which the rude wind 30
Blows in your face. I fear your disposition:
That nature which contemns its origin
Cannot be border'd certain in itself;
She that herself will sliver and disbranch
From her material sap, perforce must wither 35
And come to deadly use.
Gon. No more; the text is foolish.
Alb. Wisdom and goodness to the vile seem vile:
Filths savour but themselves. What have you done?
Tigers, not daughters, what have you perform'd? 40
A father, and a gracious aged man,
Whose reverence even the head-lugg'd bear would
    lick,
Most barbarous, most degenerate! have you
    madded.
Could my good brother suffer you to do it?
A man, a prince, by him so benefited! 45
If that the heavens do not their visible spirits
Send quickly down to tame these vile offences,
It will come,
Humanity must perforce prey on itself,
Like monsters of the deep.
Gon. Milk-liver'd man! 50
That bear'st a cheek for blows, a head for wrongs;
Who hast not in thy brows an eye discerning
Thine honour from thy suffering; that not know'st
Fools do those villains pity who are punish'd
Ere they have done their mischief. Where's thy
    drum? 55
France spreads his banners in our noiseless land,
With plumed helm thy state begins to threat,
Whiles thou, a moral fool, sit'st still and criest
'Alack, why does he so?'

ALB. See thyself, devil!
Proper deformity seems not in the fiend ₆₀
So horrid as in woman.
GON. O vain fool!
ALB. Thou changed and self-cover'd thing, for shame,
Be-monster not thy feature. Were 't my fitness
To let these hands obey my blood,
They are apt enough to dislocate and tear ₆₅
Thy flesh and bones: howe'er thou art a fiend,
A woman's shape doth shield thee.
GON. Marry, your manhood mew.

(Enter a Messenger.)

ALB. What news?
MESS. O, my good lord, the Duke of Cornwall's dead, ₇₀
Slain by his servant, going to put out
The other eye of Gloucester.
ALB. Gloucester's eyes!
MESS. A servant that he bred, thrill'd with remorse,
Opposed against the act, bending his sword
To his great master; who thereat enraged ₇₅
Flew on him and amongst them fell'd him dead,
But not without that harmful stroke which since
Hath pluck'd him after.
ALB. This shows you are above,
You justicers, that these our nether crimes
So speedily can venge. But, O poor Gloucester! ₈₀
Lost he his other eye?
MESS. Both, both, my lord.
This letter, madam, craves a speedy answer;
'Tis from your sister.
GON. *(Aside)* One way I like this well;
But being widow, and my Gloucester with her,
May all the building in my fancy pluck ₈₅
Upon my hateful life: another way,
The news is not so tart. I'll read, and answer. *(Exit.)*
ALB. Where was his son when they did take his eyes?
MESS. Come with my lady hither.
ALB. He is not here.

Mess. No, my good lord; I met him back again. 90
Alb. Knows he the wickedness?
Mess. Ay, my good lord; 'twas he inform'd against
   him,
And quit the house on purpose, that their
   punishment
Might have the freer course.
Alb. Gloucester, I live
To thank thee for the love thou show'dst the king, 95
And to revenge thine eyes. Come hither, friend:
Tell me what more thou know'st. *(Exeunt.)*

SCENE III. THE FRENCH CAMP NEAR DOVER

(Enter Kent and a Gentleman.)

Kent. Why the King of France is so suddenly gone
back know you the reason?
Gent. Something he left imperfect in the state which
since his coming forth is thought of, which imports
   to the
kingdom so much fear and danger that his personal
   return 5
was most required and necessary.
Kent. Who hath he left behind him general?
Gent. The Marshal of France, Monsieur La Far.
Kent. Did your letters pierce the queen to any
   demonstration
of grief? 10
Gent. Ay, sir; she took them, read them in my
   presence,
And now and then an ample tear trill'd down
Her delicate cheek: it seem'd she was a queen
Over her passion, who most rebel-like
Sought to be king o'er her.
Kent. O, then it moved her. 15
Gent. Not to a rage: patience and sorrow strove
Who should express her goodliest. You have seen
Sunshine and rain at once: her smiles and tears
Were like a better way: those happy smilets
That play'd on her ripe lip seem'd not to know 20
What guests were in her eyes; which parted thence
As pearls from diamonds dropp'd. In brief,

Sorrow would be a rarity most beloved,
If all could so become it.
KENT. Made she no verbal question?
GENT. Faith, once or twice she heaved the name of
    'father' 25
Pantingly forth, as if it press'd her heart;
Cried 'Sisters! sisters! Shame of ladies! sisters!
Kent! father! sisters! What, i' the storm? i' the night?
Let pity not be believed!' There she shook
The holy water from her heavenly eyes, 30
And clamour moisten'd: then away she started
To deal with grief alone.
KENT. It is the stars,
The stars above us, govern our conditions;
Else one self mate and mate could not beget
Such different issues. You spoke not with her
    since? 35
GENT. No.
KENT. Was this before the king return'd?
GENT. No, since.
KENT. Well, sir, the poor distressed Lear's i' the
    town;
Who sometime in his better tune remembers
What we are come about, and by no means 40
Will yield to see his daughter.
GENT. Why, good sir?
KENT. A sovereign shame so elbows him: his own
    unkindness
That stripp'd her from his benediction, turn'd her
To foreign casualties, gave her dear rights
To his dog-hearted daughters: these things sting 45
His mind so venomously that burning shame
Detains him from Cordelia.
GENT. Alack, poor gentleman!
KENT. Of Albany's and Cornwall's powers you
    heard not?
GENT. 'Tis so; they are afoot.
KENT. Well, sir, I'll bring you to our master Lear, 50
And leave you to attend him: some dear cause
Will in concealment wrap me up awhile;
When I am known aright, you shall not grieve
Lending me this acquaintance. I pray you, go
Along with me. *(Exeunt.)* 55

SCENE IV. THE SAME. A TENT

(Enter, with drum and colours, CORDELIA, Doctor, and Soldiers.)

COR. Alack, 'tis he: why, he was met even now
As mad as the vex'd sea; singing aloud;
Crown'd with rank fumiter and furrow-weeds,
With bur-docks, hemlock, nettles, cuckoo-flowers,
Darnel, and all the idle weeds that grow 5
In our sustaining CORN. A century send forth;
Search every acre in the high-grown field,
And bring him to our eye. *(Exit an Officer.)* What can man's wisdom
In the restoring his bereaved sense?
He that helps him take all my outward worth. 10
DOCT. There is means, madam:
Our foster-nurse of nature is repose,
The which he lacks: that to provoke in him,
Are many simples operative, whose power
Will close the eye of anguish.
COR. All blest secrets, 15
All you unpublish'd virtues of the earth,
Spring with my tears! be aidant and remediate
In the good man's distress! Seek, seek for him;
Lest his ungovern'd rage dissolve the life
That wants the means to lead it.

(Enter a Messenger.)

MESS. News, madam; 20
The British powers are marching hitherward.
COR. 'Tis known before; our preparation stands
In expectation of them. O dear father,
It is thy business that I go about;
Therefore great France 25
My mourning and important tears hath pitied.
No blown ambition doth our arms incite,
But love, dear love, and our aged father's right:
Soon may I hear and see him! *(Exeunt.)*

SCENE V. GLOUCESTER'S CASTLE

(Enter Regan and Oswald.)

Reg. But are my brother's powers set forth?
Osw. Ay, madam.
Reg. Himself in person there?
Osw. Madam, with much ado:
Your sister is the better soldier.
Reg. Lord Edmund spake not with your lord at
home?
Osw. No, madam. ₅
Reg. What might import my sister's letter to him?
Osw. I know not, lady.
Reg. Faith, he is posted hence on serious matter.
It was great ignorance, Gloucester's eyes being out,
To let him live: where he arrives he moves ₁₀
All hearts against us: Edmund, I think, is gone,
In pity of his misery, to dispatch
His nighted life; moreover, to descry
The strength o' the enemy.
Osw. I must needs after him, madam, with my
letter. ₁₅
Reg. Our troops set forth to-morrow: stay with us;
The ways are dangerous.
Osw. I may not, madam:
My lady charged my duty in this business.
Reg. Why should she write to Edmund? Might
not you
Transport her purposes by word? Belike, ₂₀
Something—I know not what: I'll love thee much,
Let me unseal the letter.
Osw. Madam, I had rather—
Reg. I know your lady does not love her husband;
I am sure of that: and at her late being here
She gave strange œillades and most speaking
looks ₂₅
To noble Edmund. I know you are of her bosom.
Osw. I, madam?
Reg. I speak in understanding: you are; I know't:
Therefore I do advise you, take this note:
My lord is dead; Edmund and I have talk'd; ₃₀
And more convenient is he for my hand

Than for your lady's: you may gather more.
If you do find him, pray you, give him this;
And when your mistress hears thus much from you,
I pray, desire her call her wisdom to her. ₃₅
So, fare you well.
If you do chance to hear of that blind traitor,
Preferment falls on him that cuts him off.
Osw. Would I could meet him, madam! I
    should show
What party I do follow.
Reg. Fare thee well. *(Exeunt.)* ₄₀

SCENE VI. FIELDS NEAR DOVER

(Enter GLOUCESTER, and EDGAR dressed like a peasant.)

Glou. When shall we come to the top of that same
    hill?
Edg. You do climb up it now: look, how we labour.
Glou. Methinks the ground is even.
Edg. Horrible steep.
Hark, do you hear the sea?
Glou. No, truly.
Edg. Why then your other senses grow imperfect ₅
By your eyes' anguish.
Glou. So may it be indeed:
Methinks thy voice is alter'd, and thou speak'st
In better phrase and matter than thou didst.
Edg. You're much deceived: in nothing am I
    changed
But in my garments.
Glou. Methinks you're better spoken. ₁₀
Edg. Come on, sir; here's the place: stand still. How
    fearful
And dizzy 'tis to cast one's eyes so low!
The crows and choughs that wing the midway air
Show scarce so gross as beetles: half way down
Hangs one that gathers samphire, dreadful trade! ₁₅
Methinks he seems no bigger than his head:
The fishermen that walk upon the beach
Appear like mice; and yond tall anchoring bark
Diminish'd to her cock; her cock, a buoy

Almost too small for sight: the murmuring surge 20
That on the unnumber'd idle pebbles chafes
Cannot be heard so high. I'll look no more,
Lest my brain turn and the deficient sight
Topple down headlong.
Glou. Set me where you stand.
Edg. Give me your hand: you are now within a
    foot 25
Of the extreme verge: for all beneath the moon
Would I not leap upright.
Glou. Let go my hand.
Here, friend, 's another purse; in it a jewel
Well worth a poor man's taking: fairies and gods
Prosper it with thee! Go thou farther off; 30
Bid me farewell, and let me hear thee going.
Edg. Now fare you well good sir.
Glou. With all my heart.
Edg. Why I do trifle thus with his despair
Is done to cure it.
Glou. (*Kneeling*) O you mighty gods!
This world I do renounce, and in your sights 35
Shake patiently my great affliction off:
If I could bear it longer and not fall
To quarrel with your great opposeless wills,
My snuff and loathed part of nature should
Burn itself out. If Edgar live, O bless him! 40
Now, fellow, fare thee well. (*He falls forward.*)
Edg. Gone, sir: farewell.
And yet I know not how conceit may rob
The treasury of life, when life itself
Yields to the theft: had he been where he thought
By this had thought been past. Alive or dead? 45
Ho, you sir! friend! Hear you, sir! speak!
Thus might he pass indeed: yet he revives.
What are you, sir?
Glou. Away, and let me die.
Edg. Hadst thou been aught but gossamer, feathers,
    air,
So many fathom down precipitating, 50
Thou'dst shiver'd like an egg: but thou dost breathe;
Hast heavy substance; bleed'st not; speak'st; art
    sound.
Ten masts at each make not the altitude

Which thou hast perpendicularly fell:
Thy life's a miracle. Speak yet again. 55
Glou. But have I fall'n, or no?
Edg. From the dread summit of this chalky bourn.
Look up a-height; the shrill-gorged lark so far
Cannot be seen or heard: do but look up.
Glou. Alack, I have no eyes. 60
Is wretchedness deprived that benefit,
To end itself by death? 'Twas yet some comfort,
When misery could beguile the tyrant's rage
And frustrate his proud will.
Edg. Give me your arm:
Up: so. How is't? Feel you your legs? You stand. 65
Glou. Too well, too well.
Edg. This is above all strangeness.
Upon the crown o' the cliff, what thing was that
Which parted from you?
Glou. A poor unfortunate beggar.
Edg. As I stood here below, methought his eyes
Were two full moons; he had a thousand noses, 70
Horns whelk'd and waved like the enridged sea:
It was some fiend; therefore, thou happy father,
Think that the clearest gods, who make them
    honours
Of men's impossibilities, have preserved thee.
Glou. I do remember now: henceforth I'll bear 75
Affliction till it do cry out itself
'Enough, enough,' and die. That thing you speak of,
I took it for a man; often 'twould say
'The fiend, the fiend:' he led me to that place.
Edg. Bear free and patient thoughts. But who comes
here? 80

(Enter Lear, fantastically dressed with wild flowers.)

The safer sense will ne'er accommodate
His master thus.
Lear. No, they cannot touch me for coining; I
    am the
king himself.
Edg. O thou side-piercing sight! 85
Lear. Nature's above art in that respect. There's
    your

press-money. That fellow handles his bow like a
    crow-keeper:
draw me a clothier's yard. Look, look, a mouse!
Peace, peace; this piece of toasted cheese will do 't.
There's my gauntlet; I'll prove it on a giant. Bring
    up 90
the brown bills. O, well flown, bird! i' the clout, i' the
clout: hewgh! Give the word.

EDG. Sweet marjoram.

LEAR. Pass.

GLOU. I know that voice. 95

LEAR. Ha! Goneril, with a white beard! They
    flattered
me like a dog, and told me I had white hairs in my
beard ere the black ones were there. To say 'ay'
    and 'no'
to every thing that I said! 'Ay' and 'no' too was
    no good
divinity. When the rain came to wet me once and the
    wind 100
to make me chatter; when the thunder would not
    peace at
my bidding; there I found 'em, there I smelt 'em
    out. Go
to, they are not men o' their words: they told me
    I was
every thing; 'tis a lie, I am not ague-proof.

GLOU. The trick of that voice I do well remember: 105
Is't not the king?

LEAR. Ay, every inch a king:
When I do stare, see how the subject quakes.
I pardon that man's life. What was thy cause?
    Adultery?
Thou shalt not die: die for adultery! No: 110
The wren goes to't, and the small gilded fly
Does lecher in my sight.
Let copulation thrive; for Gloucester's bastard son
Was kinder to his father than my daughters
Got 'tween the lawful sheets. 115
To't, luxury, pell-mell! for I lack soldiers.
Behold yond simpering dame,
Whose face between her forks presages snow,
That minces virtue and does shake the head

To hear of pleasure's name; 120
The fitchew, nor the soiled horse, goes to't
With a more riotous appetite.
Down from the waist they are Centaurs,
Though women all above:
But to the girdle do the gods inherit, 125
Beneath is all the fiends';
There's hell, there's darkness, there's the sulphurous
     pit,
Burning, scalding, stench, consumption; fie, fie,
     fie! pah,
pah! Give me an ounce of civet, good apothecary, to
sweeten my imagination: there's money for thee. 130
Glou. O, let me kiss that hand!
Lear. Let me wipe it first; it smells of mortality.
Glou. O ruin'd piece of nature! This great world
Shall so wear out to nought. Dost thou know me?
Lear. I remember thine eyes well enough. Dost
     thou 135
squiny at me? No, do thy worst, blind Cupid; I'll not
     love.
Read thou this challenge; mark but the penning on't.
Glou. Were all the letters suns, I could not see one.
Edg. I would not take this from report: it is,
And my heart breaks at it. 140
Lear. Read.
Glou. What, with the case of eyes?
Lear. O, ho, are you there with me? No eyes in your
head, nor no money in your purse? Your eyes are
     in a
heavy case, your purse in a light: yet you see how how
     this 145
world goes.
Glou. I see it feelingly.
Lear. What, art mad? A man may see how this
     world
goes with no eyes. Look with thine ears: see
     how yond
justice rails upon yond simple thief. Hark, in thine
     ear: 150
change places, and, handy-dandy, which is the
     justice, which
is the thief? Thou hast seen a farmer's dog bark at a

beggar?

GLOU. Ay, sir.

LEAR. And the creature run from the cur? There
thou ₁₅₅
mightst behold the great image of authority: a dog's
obeyed
in office.
Thou rascal beadle, hold thy bloody hand!
Why dost thou lash that whore? Strip thine own
back;
Thou hotly lust'st to use her in that kind ₁₆₀
For which thou whip'st her. The usurer hangs the
cozener.
Through tatter'd clothes small vices do appear;
Robes and furr'd gowns hide all. Plate sin with gold,
And the strong lance of justice hurtless breaks;
Arm it in rags, a pigmy's straw does pierce it. ₁₆₅
None does offend, none, I say, none; I'll able 'em:
Take that of me, my friend, who have the power
To seal the accuser's lips. Get thee glass eyes,
And, like a scurvy politician, seem
To see the things thou dost not. ₁₇₀
Now, now, now, now: pull off my boots: harder,
harder:
so.

EDG. O, matter and impertinency mix'd!
Reason in madness!

LEAR. If thou wilt weep my fortunes, take my
eyes. ₁₇₅
I know thee well enough; thy name is Gloucester:
Thou must be patient; we came crying hither:
Thou know'st, the first time that we smell the air,
We wawl and cry. I will preach to thee: mark.

GLOU. Alack, alack the day! ₁₈₀

LEAR. When we are born, we cry that we are come
To this great stage of fools. This 's a good block.
It were a delicate stratagem, to shoe
A troop of horse with felt: I'll put 't in proof;
And when I have stol'n upon these sons-in-law, ₁₈₅
Then, kill, kill, kill, kill, kill, kill!

(Enter a Gentleman, with Attendants.)

Gent. O, here he is: lay hand upon him. Sir,
Your most dear daughter—
Lear. No rescue? What, a prisoner? I am even
The natural fool of fortune. Use me well; 190
You shall have ransom. Let me have a surgeon;
I am cut to the brains.
Gent. You shall have any thing.
Lear. No seconds? all myself?
Why, this would make a man a man of salt,
To use his eyes for garden water-pots, 195
Ay, and laying autumn's dust.
Gent. Good sir,—
Lear. I will die bravely, like a smug bridegroom.
    What!
I will be jovial: come, come; I am a king,
My masters, know you that. 200
Gent. You are a royal one, and we obey you.
Lear. Then there's life in't. Nay, if you get it, you
shall get it by running. Sa, sa, sa, sa.

(Exit running; Attendants follow.)

Gent. A sight most pitiful in the meanest wretch,
Past speaking of in a king! Thou hast one daughter,
205
Who redeems nature from the general curse
Which twain have brought her to.
Edg. Hail, gentle sir.
Gent. Sir, speed you: what's your will?
Edg. Do you hear aught, sir, of a battle toward?
Gent. Most sure and vulgar: every one hears that, 210
Which can distinguish sound.
Edg. But, by your favour,
How near's the other army?
Gent. Near and on speedy foot; the main descry
Stands on the hourly thought.
Edg. I thank you, sir: that's all.
Gent. Though that the queen on special cause is
here, 215
Her army is moved on.
Edg. I thank you, sir. *(Exit Gent.)*
Glou. You ever-gentle gods, take my breath
    from me;

Let not my worser spirit tempt me again
To die before you please!
EDG. Well pray you, father.
GLOU. Now, good sir, what are you? ₂₂₀
EDG. A most poor man, made tame to fortune's
     blows;
Who, by the art of known and feeling sorrows,
Am pregnant to good pity. Give me your hand,
I'll lead you to some biding.
GLOU. Hearty thanks:
The bounty and the benison of heaven ₂₂₅
To boot, and boot!

(ENTER OSWALD.)

OSW. A proclaim'd prize! Most happy!
That eyeless head of thine was first framed flesh
To raise my fortunes. Thou old unhappy traitor,
Briefly thyself remember: the sword is out
That must destroy thee.
GLOU. Now let thy friendly hand ₂₃₀
Put strength enough to't. *(Edgar interposes.)*
OSW. Wherefore, bold peasant,
Darest thou support a publish'd traitor? Hence!
Lest that the infection of his fortune take
Like hold on thee. Let go his arm.
EDG. Chill not let go, zir, without vurther
     'casion. ₂₃₅
OSW. Let go, slave, or thou diest!
EDG. Good gentleman, go your gait, and let
     poor volk
pass. An chud ha' been zwaggered out of my life,
     'twould
not ha' been zo long as 'tis by a vortnight. Nay,
     come not
near th' old man; keep out, che vor ye, or I'se try
     whether ₂₄₀
your costard or my ballow be the harder: chill be
     plain
with you.
OSW. Out, dunghill! *(They fight.)*
EDG. Chill pick your teeth, zir: come; no matter vor
your foins. *(Oswald falls.)* ₂₄₅

Osw. Slave, thou hast slain me. Villain, take my
    purse:
If ever thou wilt thrive, bury my body;
And give the letters which thou find'st about me
To Edmund earl of Gloucester; seek him out
Upon the British party. O, untimely death! 250
Death! *(Dies.)*
Edg. I know thee well: a serviceable villain,
As duteous to the vices of thy mistress
As badness would desire.
Glou. What, is he dead?
Edg. Sit you down, father; rest you. 255
Let's see these pockets: the letters that he speaks of
May be my friends. He's dead; I am only sorry
He had no other deathsman. Let us see:
Leave, gentle wax; and, manners, blame us not:
To know our enemies' minds, we'ld rip their
    hearts; 260
Their papers, is more lawful.
(Reads) 'Let our reciprocal vows be remembered. You
have many opportunities to cut him off: if your
    will want
not, time and place will be fruitfully offered. There is
nothing done, if he return the conqueror: then am
    I 265
the prisoner, and his bed my gaol; from the loathed
warmth whereof deliver me, and supply the place
    for your
labour.
'Your—wife, so I would say—affectionate servant,
'GONERIL.' 270
O undistinguish'd space of woman's will!
A plot upon her virtuous husband's life;
And the exchange my brother! Here, in the sands,
Thee I'll rake up, the post unsanctified
Of murderous lechers; and in the mature time 275
With this ungracious paper strike the sight
Of the death-practised duke. For him 'tis well
That of thy death and business I can tell.
Glou. The king is mad: how stiff is my vile sense,
That I stand up, and have ingenious feeling 280
Of my huge sorrows! Better I were distract:
So should my thoughts be sever'd from my griefs,

And woes by wrong imaginations lose
The knowledge of themselves. *(Drum afar off.)*
EDG. Give me your hand:
Far off, methinks, I hear the beaten drum: 285
Come, father, I'll bestow you with a friend. *(Exeunt.)*

SCENE VII. A TENT IN THE FRENCH CAMP. LEAR
ON A BED ASLEEP, SOFT MUSIC PLAYING;
GENTLEMAN, AND OTHERS ATTENDING.

(Enter CORDELIA, KENT, and Doctor.)

COR. O thou good Kent, how shall I live and work,
To match thy goodness? My life will be too short,
And every measure fail me.
KENT. To be acknowledged, madam, is o'erpaid.
All my reports go with the modest truth, 5
Nor more nor clipp'd, but so.
COR. Be better suited:
These weeds are memories of those worser hours:
I prithee, put them off.
KENT. Pardon me, dear madam;
Yet to be known shortens my made intent:
My boon I make it, that you know me not 10
Till time and I think meet.
COR. Then be't so, my good lord. *(To the Doctor)*
How does the king?
DOCT. Madam, sleeps still.
COR. O you kind gods,
Cure this great breach in his abused nature! 15
The untuned and jarring senses, O, wind up
Of this child-changed father!
DOCT. So please your majesty
That we may wake the king: he hath slept long.
COR. Be govern'd by your knowledge, and proceed
I' the sway of your own will. Is he array'd? 20
GENT. Ay, madam; in the heaviness of his sleep
We put fresh garments on him.
DOCT. Be by, good madam, when we do
    awake him;
I doubt not of his temperance.
COR. Very well.

Doct. Please you, draw near. Louder the music
    there! 25
Cor. O my dear father! Restoration hang
Thy medicine on my lips, and let this kiss
Repair those violent harms that my two sisters
Have in thy reverence made!
Kent. Kind and dear princess!
Cor. Had you not been their father, these white
    flakes 30
Had challenged pity of them. Was this a face
To be opposed against the warring winds?
To stand against the deep dread-bolted thunder?
In the most terrible and nimble stroke
Of quick, cross lightning? to watch—poor
    perdu!— 35
With this thin helm? Mine enemy's dog,
Though he had bit me, should have stood that night
Against my fire; and wast thou fain, poor father,
To hovel thee with swine and rogues forlorn,
In short and musty straw? Alack, alack! 40
'Tis wonder that thy life and wits at once
Had not concluded all. He wakes; speak to him.
Doct. Madam, do you; 'tis fittest.
Cor. How does my royal lord? How fares your
    majesty?
Lear. You do me wrong to take me out o' the
    grave: 45
Thou art a soul in bliss; but I am bound
Upon a wheel of fire, that mine own tears
Do scald like molten lead.
Cor. Sir, do you know me?
Lear. You are a spirit, I know; when did you die?
Cor. Still, still, far wide! 50
Doct. He's scarce awake: let him alone awhile.
Lear. Where have I been? Where am I? Fair
    daylight?
I am mightily abused. I should e'en die with pity,
To see another thus. I know not what to say.
I will not swear these are my hands: let's see; 55
I feel this pin prick. Would I were assured
Of my condition!
Cor. O, look upon me, sir,
And hold your hands in benediction o'er me.

No, sir, you must not kneel.

LEAR. Pray, do not mock me:
I am a very foolish fond old man, 60
Fourscore and upward, not an hour more nor less;
And, to deal plainly,
I fear I am not in my perfect mind.
Methinks I should know you and know this man;
Yet I am doubtful; for I am mainly ignorant 65
What place this is, and all the skill I have
Remembers not these garments, nor I know not
Where I did lodge last night. Do not laugh at me;
For, as I am a man, I think this lady
To be my child Cordelia.

COR. And so I am, I am. 70

LEAR. Be your tears wet? yes, faith. I pray, weep not:
If you have poison for me, I will drink it.
I know you do not love me; for your sisters
Have, as I do remember, done me wrong:
You have some cause, they have not.

COR. No cause, no cause. 75

LEAR. Am I in France?

KENT. In your own kingdom, sir.

LEAR. Do not abuse me.

DOCT. Be comforted, good madam: the great rage,
You see, is kill'd in him: and yet it is danger
To make him even o'er the time he has lost. 80
Desire him to go in; trouble him no more
Till further settling.

COR. Will't please your highness walk?

LEAR. You must bear with me. Pray you now, forget
and forgive: I am old and foolish. 85

(Exeunt all but Kent and Gentleman.)

GENT. Holds it true, sir, that the Duke of Cornwall
was so slain?

KENT. Most certain, sir.

GENT. Who is conductor of his people?

KENT. As 'tis said, the bastard son of Gloucester. 90

GENT. They say Edgar, his banished son, is with the
Earl of Kent in Germany.

KENT. Report is changeable. 'Tis time to look about;
the powers of the kingdom approach apace.

GENT. The arbitrement is like to be bloody. Fare
    you 95
well, sir. *(Exit.)*
KENT. My point and period will be throughly
    wrought,
Or well or ill, as this day's battle's fought. *(Exit.)*

ACT V.

*(Enter, with drum and colours, EDMUND, REGAN, Gentlemen,
and Soldiers.)*

EDM. Know of the duke if his last purpose hold,
Or whether since he is advised by aught
To change the course: he's full of alteration
And self-reproving: bring his constant pleasure.

(To a Gentleman, who goes out.)

REG. Our sister's man is certainly miscarried. ₅
EDM. 'Tis to be doubted, madam.
REG. Now, sweet lord,
You know the goodness I intend upon you:
Tell me, but truly, but then speak the truth,
Do you not love my sister?
EDM. In honour'd love.
REG. But have you never found my brother's way ₁₀
To the forfended place?
EDM. That thought abuses you.
REG. I am doubtful that you have been conjunct
And bosom'd with her, as far as we call hers.
EDM. No, by mine honour, madam.
REG. I never shall endure her: dear my lord, ₁₅
Be not familiar with her.

EDM. Fear me not.——
She and the duke her husband!

(Enter, with drum and colours, ALBANY, GONERIL, and Soldiers.)

GON. (Aside) I had rather lose the battle than that
    sister
Should loosen him and me.
ALB. Our very loving sister, well be-met. 20
Sir, this I hear; the king is come to his daughter,
With others whom the rigour of our state
Forced to cry out. Where I could not be honest,
I never yet was valiant: for this business,
It toucheth us, as France invades our land, 25
Not bolds the king, with others, whom, I fear,
Most just and heavy causes make oppose.
EDM. Sir, you speak nobly.
REG. Why is this reason'd?
GON. Combine together 'gainst the enemy;
For these domestic and particular broils 30
Are not the question here.
ALB. Let's then determine
With the ancient of war on our proceedings.
EDM. I shall attend you presently at your tent.
REG. Sister, you'll go with us?
GON. No. 35
REG. 'Tis most convenient; pray you, go with us.
GON. (Aside) O, ho, I know the riddle.——I will go.

(As they are going out, enter EDGAR disguised.)

EDG. If e'er your grace had speech with man so poor,
Hear me one word.
ALB. I'll overtake you. Speak.

(Exeunt all but Albany and Edgar.)

EDG. Before you fight the battle, ope this letter. 40
If you have victory, let the trumpet sound
For him that brought it: wretched though I seem,
I can produce a champion that will prove
What is avouched there. If you miscarry,
Your business of the world hath so an end, 45

And machination ceases. Fortune love you!
ALB. Stay till I have read the letter.
EDG. I was forbid it.
When time shall serve, let but the herald cry,
And I'll appear again.
ALB. Why, fare thee well: I will o'erlook thy paper. 50

(Exit Edgar.)

(Re-enter EDMUND.)

EDM. The enemy's in view: draw up your powers.
Here is the guess of their true strength and forces
By diligent discovery; but your haste
Is now urged on you.
ALB. We will greet the time. *(Exit.)*
EDM. To both these sisters have I sworn my love; 55
Each jealous of the other, as the stung
Are of the adder. Which of them shall I take?
Both? one? or neither? Neither can be enjoy'd,
If both remain alive: to take the widow
Exasperates, makes mad her sister Goneril; 60
And hardly shall I carry out my side,
Her husband being alive. Now then we'll use
His countenance for the battle; which being done,
Let her who would be rid of him devise
His speedy taking off. As for the mercy 65
Which he intends to Lear and to Cordelia,
The battle done, and they within our power,
Shall never see his pardon; for my state
Stands on me to defend, not to debate. *(Exit.)*

SCENE II. A FIELD BETWEEN THE TWO CAMPS.

*(Alarum within. Enter, with drum and colours, Lear, CORDELIA,
and Soldiers, over the stage; and exeunt.)*
(ENTER EDGAR AND GLOUCESTER.)

EDG. Here, father, take the shadow of this tree
For your good host; pray that the right may thrive:
If ever I return to you again,
I'll bring you comfort.
GLOU. Grace go with you, sir! *(Exit Edgar.)*

(Alarum and retreat within. Re-enter EDGAR.)

EDG. Away, old man; give me thy hand; away! ₅
King Lear hath lost, he and his daughter ta'en:
Give me thy hand; come on.
GLOU. No farther, sir; a man may rot even here.
EDG. What, in ill thoughts again? Men must endure
Their going hence, even as their coming hither: ₁₀
Ripeness is all: come on.
GLOU. And that's true too. *(Exeunt.)*

SCENE III. THE BRITISH CAMP NEAR DOVER

*(Enter, in conquest, with drum and colours, EDMUND; LEAR and
CORDELIA, as prisoners; Captain, Soldiers, &c.)*

EDM. Some officers take them away: good guard,
Until their greater pleasures first be known
That are to censure them.
COR. We are not the first
Who with best meaning have incurr'd the worst.
For thee, oppressed king, am I cast down; ₅
Myself could else out-frown false fortune's frown.
Shall we not see these daughters and these sisters?
LEAR. No, no, no, no! Come, let's away to prison:
We two alone will sing like birds i' the cage:
When thou dost ask me blessing, I'll kneel down ₁₀
And ask of thee forgiveness: so we'll live,
And pray, and sing, and tell old tales, and laugh
At gilded butterflies, and hear poor rogues
Talk of court news; and we'll talk with them too,
Who loses and who wins, who's in, who's out; ₁₅
And take upon's the mystery of things,
As if we were God's spies: and we'll wear out,
In a wall'd prison, packs and sects of great ones
That ebb and flow by the moon.
EDM. Take them away.
LEAR. Upon such sacrifices, my Cordelia, ₂₀
The gods themselves throw incense. Have I caught
    thee?
He that parts us shall bring a brand from heaven,
And fire us hence like foxes. Wipe thine eyes;
The good-years shall devour them, flesh and fell,

Ere they shall make us weep: we'll see 'em starve
    first. 25
Come. *(Exeunt Lear and Cordelia, guarded.)*
EDM. Come hither, captain; hark.
Take thou this note: go follow them to prison:
One step I have advanced thee; if thou dost
As this instructs thee, thou dost make thy way 30
To noble fortunes: know thou this, that men
Are as the time is: to be tender-minded
Does not become a sword: thy great employment
Will not bear question; either say thou'lt do 't,
Or thrive by other means.
CAPT. I'll do 't, my lord. 35
EDM. About it; and write happy when thou hast
    done.
Mark, I say, instantly, and carry it so
As I have set it down.
CAPT. I cannot draw a cart, nor eat dried oats;
If it be man's work, I'll do 't. *(Exit.)* 40

*(Flourish. Enter ALBANY, GONERIL, REGAN, another Captain,
and Soldiers.)*

ALB. Sir, you have shown to-day your valiant strain,
And fortune led you well: you have the captives
That were the opposites of this day's strife:
We do require them of you, so to use them
As we shall find their merits and our safety 45
May equally determine.
EDM. Sir, I thought it fit
To send the old and miserable king
To some retention and appointed guard;
Whose age has charms in it, whose title more,
To pluck the common bosom on his side, 50
And turn our impress'd lances in our eyes
Which do command them. With him I sent the
    queen:
My reason all the same; and they are ready
To-morrow or at further space to appear
Where you shall hold your session. At this time 55
We sweat and bleed: the friend hath lost his friend;
And the best quarrels, in the heat, are cursed
By those that feel their sharpness.

The question of Cordelia and her father
Requires a fitter place.
ALB. Sir, by your patience, 60
I hold you but a subject of this war,
Not as a brother.
REG. That's as we list to grace him.
Methinks our pleasure might have been demanded,
Ere you had spoke so far. He led our powers,
Bore the commission of my place and person; 65
The which immediacy may well stand up
And call itself your brother.
GON. Not so hot:
In his own grace he doth exalt himself
More than in your addition.
REG. In my rights,
By me invested, he compeers the best. 70
GON. That were the most, if he should husband you.
REG. Jesters do oft prove prophets.
GON. Holla, holla!
That eye that told you so look'd but a-squint.
REG. Lady, I am not well; else I should answer
From a full-flowing stomach. General,
Take thou my soldiers, prisoners, patrimony;
Dispose of them, of me; the walls are thine:
Witness the world, that I create thee here
My lord and master.
GON. Mean you to enjoy him?
ALB. The let-alone lies not in your good will. 80
EDM. Nor in thine, lord.
ALB. Half-blooded fellow, yes.
REG. *(To Edmund)* Let the drum strike, and prove my
title thine.
ALB. Stay yet; hear reason. Edmund, I arrest thee
On capital treason; and in thine attaint
This gilded serpent *(Pointing to GON.)*. For your
claim, fair sister, 85
I bar it in the interest of my wife;
'Tis she is sub-contracted to this lord,
And I, her husband, contradict your bans.
If you will marry, make your loves to me;
My lady is bespoke.
GON. An interlude! 90

ALB. Thou art arm'd, Gloucester: let the trumpet
    sound:
If none appear to prove upon thy person
Thy heinous, manifest, and many treasons,
There is my pledge *(Throwing down a glove)*: I'll prove
    it on thy heart,
Ere I taste bread, thou art in nothing less ₉₅
Than I have here proclaim'd thee.
REG. Sick, O, sick!
GON. (Aside) If not, I'll ne'er trust medicine.
EDM. (Throwing down a glove) There's my exchange:
    what in the world he is
That names me traitor, villain-like he lies:
Call by thy trumpet: he that dares approach, ₁₀₀
On him, on you,—who not?—I will maintain
My truth and honour firmly.
ALB. A herald, ho!
EDM. A herald, ho, a herald!
ALB. Trust to thy single virtue; for thy soldiers,
All levied in my name, have in my name ₁₀₅
Took their discharge.
REG. My sickness grows upon me.
ALB. She is not well; convey her to my tent.

                  (Exit Regan, led.)

      (Enter a Herald.)

Come hither, herald,—Let the trumpet sound,—
And read out this.
CAPT. Sound, trumpet! *(A trumpet sounds.)* ₁₁₀
HER. (Reads) 'If any man of quality or degree within
the lists of the army will maintain upon Edmund,
    supposed
Earl of Gloucester, that he is a manifold traitor,
    let him
appear by the third sound of the trumpet: he is
    bold in
his defence.' ₁₁₅
EDM. Sound! *(First trumpet.)*
HER. Again! *(Second trumpet.)*
HER. Again! *(Third trumpet.)*

(Trumpet answers within.)

(Enter EDGAR, at the third sound, armed, with a trumpet before him.)

ALB. Ask him his purposes, why he appears
Upon this call o' the trumpet.
HER. What are you? 120
Your name, your quality? and why you answer
This present summons?
EDG. Know, my name is lost;
By treason's tooth bare-gnawn and canker-bit:
Yet am I noble as the adversary
I come to cope.
ALB. Which is that adversary? 125
EDG. What's he that speaks for Edmund, Earl of
     Gloucester?
EDM. Himself: what say'st thou to him?
EDG. Draw thy sword,
That if my speech offend a noble heart,
Thy arm may do thee justice: here is mine.
Behold, it is the privilege of mine honours, 130
My oath, and my profession: I protest,
Maugre thy strength, youth, place and eminence,
Despite thy victor sword and fire-new fortune,
Thy valour and thy heart, thou art a traitor,
False to thy gods, thy brother and thy father, 135
Conspirant 'gainst this high illustrious prince,
And from the extremest upward of thy head
To the descent and dust below thy foot,
A most toad-spotted traitor. Say thou 'No,'
This sword, this arm and my best spirits are bent 140
To prove upon thy heart, whereto I speak,
Thou liest.
EDM. In wisdom I should ask thy name,
But since thy outside looks so fair and warlike
And that thy tongue some say of breeding breathes,
What safe and nicely I might well delay 145
By rule of knighthood, I disdain and spurn:
Back do I toss these treasons to thy head;
With the hell-hated lie o'erwhelm thy heart;
Which for they yet glance by and scarcely bruise,
This sword of mine shall give them instant way, 150

Where they shall rest for ever. Trumpets, speak!

(Alarums. They fight. Edmund falls.)

ALB. Save him, save him!
GON. This is practice, Gloucester:
By the law of arms thou wast not bound to answer
An unknown opposite; thou art not vanquish'd,
But cozen'd and beguiled.
ALB. Shut your mouth, dame, 155
Or with this paper shall I stop it. Hold, sir;
Thou worse than any name, read thine own evil.
No tearing, lady; I perceive you know it.
GON. Say, if I do, the laws are mine, not thine:
Who can arraign me for't?
ALB. Most monstrous! 160
Know'st thou this paper?
GON. Ask me not what I know. *(Exit.)*
ALB. Go after her: she's desperate; govern her.
EDM. What you have charged me with, that have I
    done;
And more, much more; the time will bring it out:
'Tis past, and so am I. But what art thou 165
That hast this fortune on me? If thou'rt noble,
I do forgive thee.
EDG. Let's exchange charity.
I am no less in blood than thou art, Edmund;
If more, the more thou hast wrong'd me.
My name is Edgar, and thy father's son. 170
The gods are just, and of our pleasant vices
Make instruments to plague us:
The dark and vicious place where thee he got
Cost him his eyes.
EDM. Thou hast spoken right, 'tis true;
The wheel is come full circle; I am here. 175
ALB. Methought thy very gait did prophesy
A royal nobleness: I must embrace thee:
Let sorrow split my heart, if ever I
Did hate thee or thy father!
EDG. Worthy prince, I know't.
ALB. Where have you hid yourself? 180
How have you known the miseries of your father?
EDG. By nursing them, my lord. List a brief tale;

And when 'tis told, O, that my heart would burst!
The bloody proclamation to escape
That follow'd me so near,—O, our lives' sweetness!
That we the pain of death would hourly die   185
Rather than die at once!—taught me to shift
Into a madman's rags, to assume a semblance
That very dogs disdain'd: and in this habit
Met I my father with his bleeding rings,   190
Their precious stones new lost; became his guide,
Led him, begg'd for him, saved him from despair;
Never—O fault!—reveal'd myself unto him,
Until some half-hour past, when I was arm'd;
Not sure, though hoping, of this good success,   195
I ask'd his blessing, and from first to last
Told him my pilgrimage: but his flaw'd heart,—
Alack, too weak the conflict to support!—
'Twixt two extremes of passion, joy and grief,
Burst smilingly.
EDM. This speech of yours hath moved me,   200
And shall perchance do good: but speak you on;
You look as you had something more to say.
ALB. If there be more, more woful, hold it in;
For I am almost ready to dissolve,
Hearing of this.
EDG. This would have seem'd a period   205
To such as love not sorrow; but another,
To amplify too much, would make much more,
And top extremity.
Whilst I was big in clamour, came there in a man,
Who, having seen me in my worst estate,   210
Shunn'd my abhorr'd society; but then, finding
Who 'twas that so endured, with his strong arms
He fasten'd on my neck, and bellow'd out
As he'ld burst heaven; threw him on my father;
Told the most piteous tale of Lear and him   215
That ever ear received: which in recounting
His grief grew puissant, and the strings of life
Began to crack: twice then the trumpets sounded,
And there I left him tranced.
ALB. But who was this?
EDG. Kent, sir, the banish'd Kent; who in disguise   220
Follow'd his enemy king, and did him service

Improper for a slave.

(Enter a Gentleman, with a bloody knife.)

GENT. Help, help, O, help!
EDG. What kind of help?
ALB. Speak, man.
EDG. What means this bloody knife?
GENT. 'Tis hot, it smokes;
It came even from the heart of—O, she's dead! 225
ALB. Who dead? speak, man.
GENT. Your lady, sir, your lady: and her sister
By her is poisoned; she hath confess'd it.
EDM. I was contracted to them both: all three
Now marry in an instant.
EDG. Here comes KENT. 230
ALB. Produce the bodies, be they alive or dead.

(Exit Gentleman.)

This judgement of the heavens, that makes us
tremble,
Touches us not with pity.

(Enter KENT.)

O, is this he?
The time will not allow the compliment
Which very manners urges.
KENT. I am come 235
To bid my king and master aye good night:
Is he not here?
ALB. Great thing of us forgot!
Speak, Edmund, where's the king? and where's
Cordelia?
See'st thou this object, Kent?

(The bodies of Gonerll and Regan are brought in.)

KENT. Alack, why thus?
EDM. Yet Edmund was beloved: 240
The one the other poison'd for my sake,
And after slew herself.

Alb. Even so. Cover their faces.
Edm. I pant for life: some good I mean to do,
Despite of mine own nature. Quickly send, ₂₄₅
Be brief in it, to the castle; for my writ
Is on the life of Lear and on Cordelia:
Nay, send in time.
Alb. Run, run, O, run!
Edg. To who, my lord? Who hath the office? send
Thy token of reprieve. ₂₅₀
Edm. Well thought on: take my sword,
Give it the captain.
Alb. Haste thee, for thy life. *(Exit Edgar.)*
Edm. He hath commission from thy wife and me
To hang Cordelia in the prison, and
To lay the blame upon her own despair, ₂₅₅
That she fordid herself.
Alb. The gods defend her! Bear him hence awhile.

(Edmund is borne off.)

(Re-enter Lear, *with* Cordelia *dead in his arms;* Edgar,
Captain, and others following.)

Lear. Howl, howl, howl, howl! O, you are men of
stones:
Had I your tongues and eyes, I'ld use them so
That heaven's vault should crack. She's gone for
ever! ₂₆₀
I know when one is dead and when one lives;
She's dead as earth. Lend me a looking-glass;
If that her breath will mist or stain the stone,
Why, then she lives.
Kent. Is this the promised end?
Edg. Or image of that horror?
Alb. Fall and cease. ₂₆₅
Lear. This feather stirs; she lives. If it be so,
It is a chance which does redeem all sorrows
That ever I have felt.
Kent. (Kneeling) O my good master!
Lear. Prithee, away.
Edg. 'Tis noble Kent, your friend.
Lear. A plague upon you, murderers, traitors all! ₂₇₀
I might have saved her; now she's gone for ever!

Cordelia, Cordelia! stay a little. Ha!
What is't thou say'st? Her voice was ever soft,
Gentle and low, an excellent thing in woman.
I kill'd the slave that was a-hanging thee. ₂₇₅
CAPT. 'Tis true, my lords, he did.
LEAR. Did I not, fellow?
I have seen the day, with my good biting falchion
I would have made them skip: I am old now,
And these same crosses spoil me. Who are you?
Mine eyes are not o' the best: I'll tell you straight. ₂₈₀
KENT. If fortune brag of two she loved and hated,
One of them we behold.
LEAR. This is a dull sight. Are you not Kent?
KENT. The same,
Your servant *KENT.* Where is your servant Caius?
LEAR. He's a good fellow, I can tell you that; ₂₈₅
He'll strike, and quickly too: he's dead and rotten.
KENT. No, my good lord; I am the very man—
LEAR. I'll see that straight.
KENT. That from your first of difference and decay
Have follow'd your sad steps.
LEAR. You are welcome hither. ₂₉₀
KENT. Nor no man else: all's cheerless, dark and
        deadly.
Your eldest daughters have fordone themselves.
And desperately are dead.
LEAR. Ay, so I think.
ALB. He knows not what he says, and vain is it
That we present us to him.
EDG. Very bootless. ₂₉₅

(Enter a Captain.)

CAPT. Edmund is dead, my lord.
ALB. That's but a trifle here.
You lords and noble friends, know our intent.
What comfort to this great decay may come
Shall be applied: for us, we will resign,
During the life of this old majesty, ₃₀₀
To him our absolute power: *(To Edgar and Kent)* you,
        to your rights;
With boot, and such addition as your honours
Have more than merited. All friends shall taste

The wages of their virtue, and all foes
The cup of their deservings. O, see, see! 305
LEAR. And my poor fool is hang'd! No, no, no life!
Why should a dog, a horse, a rat, have life,
And thou no breath at all? Thou'lt come no more,
Never, never, never, never, never!
Pray you, undo this button: thank you, sir. 310
Do you see this? Look on her, look, her lips,
Look there, look there! *(Dies.)*
EDG. He faints. My lord, my lord!
KENT. Break, heart; I prithee, break!
EDG. Look up, my lord.
KENT. Vex not his ghost: O, let him pass! he
    hates him
That would upon the rack of this tough world 315
Stretch him out longer.
EDG. He is gone indeed.
KENT. The wonder is he hath endured so long:
He but usurp'd his life.
ALB. Bear them from hence. Our present business
Is general woe. *(To Kent and Edgar)* Friends of my
    soul, you twain 320
Rule in this realm and the gored state sustain.
KENT. I have a journey, sir, shortly to go;
My master calls me, I must not say no.
ALB. The weight of this sad time we must obey,
Speak what we feel, not what we ought to say. 325
The oldest hath borne most: we that are young
Shall never see so much, nor live so long.

(Exeunt, with a dead march.)